The Territorial Dimension
of Judaism

ABOUT
QUANTUM
BOOKS

QUANTUM, THE UNIT OF
EMITTED ENERGY. A QUANTUM
BOOK IS A SHORT STUDY
DISTINCTIVE FOR THE AUTHOR'S
ABILITY TO OFFER A RICHNESS OF
DETAIL AND INSIGHT WITHIN
ABOUT ONE HUNDRED PAGES
OF PRINT. SHORT ENOUGH TO BE
READ IN AN EVENING AND
SIGNIFICANT ENOUGH
TO BE A BOOK

W. D. Davies

The Territorial Dimension of Judaism

University of California Press

Berkeley · *Los Angeles* · *London*

University of California Press
Berkeley and Los Angeles, California

University of California Press, Ltd.
London, England

© 1982 by
The Regents of the University of California

Library of Congress Cataloging in Publication Data
Davies, William David, 1911–
    The territorial dimension of Judaism.
    Bibliography: p.
    Includes index.
    1. Palestine in the Bible. 2. Palestine in
Judaism. I. Title.
BS1199.P26D38   296.3'877   81–53
ISBN 0–520–04331–6   AACR1

35, 122

Printed in the United States of America

1 2 3 4 5 6 7 8 9

To my colleagues and students
in the Divinity School and the Department of Religion
of Duke University

Contents

List of Abbreviations

Abbreviations of books from the Old Testament (Tanak) and from the New Testament will be familiar to readers and hence are not listed.

APOT: R. H. Charles (ed.), *The Apocrypha and Pseudepigrapha of the Old Testament*

BT: The Babylonian Talmud.

DJD I: D. Barthélemy, O.P., et al., *Qumran Cave I: Discoveries in the Judaean Desert,* I

GL: W. D. Davies, *The Gospel and the Land: Early Christianity . and Jewish Territorial Doctrine*

JEDPH: The materials that went into the making of the Pentateuch (the first five books of the Tanak).

J: The source or tradition from the south, using the name *Yahweh* (Jehovah) for God, dating from the eleventh to the early eighth century B.C.E.

E: A source or tradition coming from the north, also dating from the eleventh to the early eighth century B.C.E., using the term *Elohim* for God. Probably fused with J into one complex after 722 B.C.E.

D: Deuteronomy, dating in its earliest form from the seventh century B.C.E.

P: The Priestly Code of the postexilic or Persian period, dealing with cultic laws and the history of the cult

H: The Holiness Code (Lev. 17–26), dated
600–570 B.C.E., emphasizing holiness, The
Land as polluted by sin, sacrifices, the duties of priests, and the calendar. Emerged
between *D* and *P*, to which it seems related

LXX: *The Septuagint*, the Greek version of the
Hebrew Old Testament

NEB: *The New English Bible*

RSV: *The Revised Standard Version of the Bible*

Apocrypha and Pseudepigrapha (see Charles, *Apocrypha and
Pseudepigrapha of the Old Testament*)

Asmp. M.: The Assumption of Moses

2 Bar.: 2 (or Syriac) Baruch. Greek or Hebrew,
from Palestine, ca. 90 C.E.

Ecclus.: Ecclesiasticus, or The Wisdom of Jesus ben
[the son of] Sirach. Hebrew, from Palestine
(Jerusalem?). Ben Sirach wrote the Hebrew
text ca. 180 B.C.E. His grandson translated
it into Greek ca. 130 B.C.E.

1 En.: 1 Enoch or Ethiopic Enoch. Hebrew and/or
Aramaic, from Jerusalem (?), of composite
date (ca. 150 B.C.E.–early first century C.E.)

4 Ezra: Also known as 2 Esdras. Greek version is a
translation from Hebrew or Aramaic. Palestinian, ca. 90–100 C.E.

Jub.: Jubilees or Little Genesis. Hebrew, from
Palestine, second century B.C.E. Essene?

1 Macc.: 1 Maccabees. The present Greek text is a
translation from Hebrew. Probably written
ca. 100 B.C.E.

2 Macc.: Not a continuation of 1 Maccabees. In its
present form, presumably produced in Alexandria ca. 50 B.C.E. Based on the lost
history of Jason of Cyrene

Ps. Sol.: Psalms of Solomon. Hebrew, from Palestine, ca. 50 B.C.E.

Sib. Or.: Sibylline Oracles. Greek, from Alexandria.

Bk. 3 ca. 150 B.C.E.; bk. 4, ca. 80 C.E.; bk. 5, ca. 100–150 C.E.

Test.Ab.: Testament of Abraham. Hebrew (but the Greek does not read like a translation), early first century C.E.

Test.Job: Testament of Job. Greek, perhaps from Alexandria, first century B.C.E. or first century C.E.

Test.Levi: Testament of Levi. In its present form, a Christian composition of the second century C.E., but based on a Jewish Palestinian text from the second century B.C.E.

Tob.: Tobit. Hebrew or Aramaic, ca. 200 B.C.E. Egypt or Western Syria has been suggested as the provenance: Babylon and Palestine have not been ruled out (text does have Persian influences)

Wisd. Sol.: Wisdom of Solomon. Greek, reflecting the syle of the Septuagint from Alexandria, second or first century B.C.E.

Texts from the Dead Sea Scrolls

11QPs[a]: Manuscript from cave 11, Qumran, containing forty-one canonical psalms and several apocryphal psalms

CDC: The Damascus Rule. Preserved in two medieval manuscripts. Fragments have also been found at Qumran

1QS: The Manual of Discipline from cave I, Qumran

1QpHab and 1QpH: The commentary on Habakkuk from cave I (*péšer Habakkuk*)

1QIsa[a]: A scroll of Isaiah from cave I, Qumran, exemplar *a*

1QM: The sectarian War of the Children of Light against the Children of Darkness (*milḥāmāh*)

4Q Flor.: 4 Q Florilegium. Published by J. Allegro in

the *Journal of Biblical Literature* in 1956 and 1958

For introduction and English translation of the Dead Sea Scrolls, see G. Vermes, *The Dead Sea Scrolls in English*. The Temple Scroll referred to herein has not been translated into English: for an introduction to it see J. Milgrom, "The Temple Scroll"; German translation: J. Maier, *Die Tempelrolle vom Toten Meer*; French translation: A. Caquot, "Le Rouleau du Temple de Qoumran."

Preface

In 1967, just before the Six Days' War between Israel and Egypt, a letter came from Jerusalem urging my support for the cause of Israel. It was informed by assumptions that, despite my immersion for years in the study of Judaism, I had never fully faced, and it compelled a deep examination of what is—I soon realized—the Cinderella of both Christian and Jewish scholarship: the theme of territory in Judaism. The result was *The Gospel and The Land: Early Christianity and Jewish Territorial Doctrine*, published by the University of California Press in 1974. But the subject continued to burn in my bones like a fire, and this short book carries on the consideration of the territorial theme, this time exclusively in Judaism, against the larger context of Jewish history since the first and second centuries C.E. There is here no attempt to deal with the specifically Christian response to the theme.

What happens when the understanding of The Promised Land in Judaism conflicts with the claims of the traditions and occupancy of its other peoples is also not discussed here. From different points of view, my friends and mentors Professor David Daube and Dr. J. S. Whale, who, were it necessary, would have made it impossible for me to underestimate the tragedy of the conflict between Israelis and Palestinians, have urged me to deal with it. From their criticisms I have greatly profited. However, apart from the question of competence, to engage that issue would demand another volume. Here I have concentrated on what in my judgement must be the beginning for an understanding of this conflict: the sympathetic attempt to comprehend the Jewish tradition. This is the justification for my brief study, which is designed primarily, first, to introduce the subject for discussion among a wide public, and secondly, since the territorial theme touches upon matters beyond the competence of any one student, to stimulate specialists to consider this much-neglected subject now forcing itself upon the world's attention.

My warmest gratitude goes to Professors D. N. Freedman and Jacob Neusner and to my colleagues Martin Golding and Edward Tiryakian; to Mr. Dale C. Allison, my assistant, for much valuable stimulus, and Mr. Richard Countie, for help in the final stages; to my secretary, Mrs. Sarah Freedman, for her interested help; especially to the Librarian of Duke Divinity School, Professor Donn M. Farris, who seems always to go beyond the call of duty, and to his staff, particularly Ms. Harriet Leonard and Ms. Linda K. Gard; and to Mr. Richard Judd and Mr. George Mandel of the Oxford Centre for Postgraduate Hebrew Studies. I wish to acknowledge the help and concern of Mr. William J. McClung, Executive Editor in Berkeley, and the extraordinary efficiency of Ms. Marilyn Schwartz and Mr. Peter Dreyer, editor and reader for the Press. My debt to my wife, in this as in all my endeavours, cannot adequately be expressed and I do not attempt it.

W. D. D.

Duke University
February 3, 1981

Introductory

This volume attempts to answer the question whether there is an essential territorial dimension to Judaism. Put concretely, it assesses the nature and place within Judaism of the doctrine which in various ways asserts that there is a special relationship among the God of Israel, the People of Israel, and The Land of Israel. Is that relationship primary or secondary, dispensable or indispensable? Is the territorial doctrine of Judaism accidental and peripheral or essential, an aspect of Judaism without which Judaism would cease to be itself?

At first encounter the question would seem to be open to strict historical investigation and an unequivocal answer. However difficult, the sources for understanding Judaism are abundant: the practice of Jews as it bears upon Eretz Israel[1] is open to scrutiny. But in the course of Jewish history especially in this century, internal and external factors affecting Judaism have clouded as well as clarified the issue and compel caution. The complexities, paradoxes,

---

1. Two Hebrew terms are translatable as "land," and in some cases have a similar meaning, but they are not identical: *'adâmâh* primarily designates the land as habitable, without political or national connotations; *'eretz* can, and very often does, have such a connotation. It is with Eretz Israel (henceforth The Land), with that connotation, that we are concerned here. The Land was never defined with geographic precision. See W. D. Davies, *The Gospel and The Land* (henceforth *GL*), p. 16, n. 3, and p. 73; also N. Avigad and Y. Yadin, eds., *The Genesis Apocryphon*, col. 21, lines 15–18, pp. 45–46.

and obscurities of the territorial theme cannot be sufficiently emphasized.

Besides the inherent difficulty of the sources and the factors at which we have hinted, there is another reason the question of The Land remains one of the most neglected aspects of Judaism: the contemporary approach of Gentile (largely Christian) scholarship and also, by way of reaction to this, of much Jewish scholarship, to the Jewish tradition. Christian origins have usually been approached in two ways. One approach, bearing the authority of a long history and renewed with vigour in this century, has emphasized the radical newness of the Gospel as a supernatural phenomenon breaking into this world with startling discontinuity in a manner that defies rational analysis. The other approach, more characteristic of the nineteenth and early twentieth centuries, has sought to understand the emergence of the Christian faith as a phenomenon within history which, partly at least, can be interpreted in relation to contemporary religions. This second approach has forked in two directions, one leading to the Graeco-Roman world and one to the Jewish: and the Christian faith has correspondingly been illumined in terms either of Hellenistic syncretism or of the Judaism of the first century. Only in recent decades have scholars recognized that the Hellenistic and Judaic cultures and religions of the period reveal deep interpenetration.

Even when Christian origins are understood in the Hellenistic and Jewish setting, Christian scholars have usually determined how that setting is used and what aspects of it are significant for the illumination of the Christian faith. This is especially true of the way Judaism has been examined as a background to Christianity. Long before the emergence of modern scholarship, the pagan faiths of the Graeco-Roman world that vied with Christianity for the allegiance of men in the first century had died. But because Judaism has persisted as a living faith to the present, a peculiarly contemporaneous relevance and urgency have always characterized the discussion of the relationship between it and Christianity. One might expect that Judaism would have helped formulate the terms of the discussion between the two faiths. In fact, because of the overwhelming dominance of Christianity, the discussion has been governed almost entirely by concerns Christians have deemed important. Despite their emphasis on the Word made flesh (that is, "material"), doctrines in which Christians have been particularly interested—theological and metaphysical abstractions such as God, Creation, Time, Man, Sin, Revelation, Prophecy, Reward, and Punishment—have been emphasized in attempts to understand how the Gospel emerged from and impinged upon Judaism. The Jewish faith came to be understood largely in terms of Christian categories, seldom in terms native, or peculiar, to itself. And once Judaism came to be interpreted as a body of ideas or doctrines, the assumption followed that its ideas, to be true, must be valid for all persons at all times and places. Local or geographic, particularistic elements in Judaism could be disregarded as insignificant—or, at best, secondary.

This explains why the question of The Land in primitive Christianity has been neglected. Even rabbinic theology, borrowing its philosophical tools and methods from, and stimulated by, Christian theology, concentrated on themes dictated by the need to defend itself against specifically Christian challenges, and neglected such awkward, particular doctrines as that of The Land. Rabbinic thinkers, understanding Judaism in terms of, or in reaction to, Christianity, did not appreciate what significance a particular place, Palestine, could have in their faith: and Christian

scholars, naturally governed by their own doctrinal interests, easily neglected the *realia* of Judaism and especially its
traditional concentration on The Land. So it is that neither
the *Interpreter's Dictionary of the Bible*, published in 1962,
nor two recent French biblical dictionaries contain articles
on The Land. *The Peake Commentary* (1962) has two references to the theme in its index: *The Jerome Biblical Commentary* (1968) virtually ignores it; and the *Wörterbuch* of Kittel-
Friedrich (1933) allots just under four pages to it. Although
there are innumerable references to The Land in the document of their concern, until very recently the neglect of this
theme has been as marked among scholars of the Tanak
(the term used by Jews for what Protestant Christians call
the Old Testament) as among those of the New Testament.

But, despite its comparative neglect until recently, even
in formal rabbinic theology, the emphasis on The Land in
Judaism is one of the most persistent and passionately held
doctrines with which the early Church had to come to
terms. The doctrine is traceable throughout the Tanak, the
Apocrypha and Pseudepigrapha, the Qumran Scrolls, and
the rabbinic and Hellenistic Jewish sources.

1
A Marked Theological Tradition

The Tanak and other sources of Judaism reveal certain ideas concerning The Land that reflect, or are parallel to, primitive Semitic, other Near Eastern, and, indeed, widespread conceptions about the significance of their land to a particular people. Israel is represented as the centre of the earth. Mircea Eliade has connected this notion with that of sacred and profane space, which is common in human societies. Sacred space is that space which has manifested an irruption of the divine, and which alone, therefore, is real or possesses being. The religious man desires to live as near to this sacred space as possible and comes to regard it, the place of his abode, his own land, as the centre of the world. To this belongs cosmos, order: outside it is chaos, where demons and alien spirits rule.

The belief that The Land of Israel is the centre of the earth occurs in Ezek. 38:12. In the end of days, when many people out of the nations will have been gathered upon the mountains of Israel to dwell in security, Gog, of the land of Magog, is to advance against them. The people of Israel are described as those

> who dwell at the centre of the earth.

This notion also emerges in Ezek. 5:5: "Thus says the Lord God: This is Jerusalem; I have set her in the centre of the nations, with countries round about her." Here the emphasis is demographic—that is, on the visibility of the conduct of Jerusalem to all the nations of the world because of her centrality. The idea persisted, as in the Ethiopic Enoch 26:1, where Enoch's visit to Jerusalem is described as his going to "the middle of earth." In Jub. 8:12, Noah assigns to Shem as his lot, "the centre of the earth." We learn what this is explicitly in Jub. 8:19, where Mount Zion is described as "the centre of the navel [*omphalos*] of the earth." The context of these verses is geographic, the division of the earth among the sons of Noah. But the centrality of Jerusalem is connected also with other holy places—the Garden of Eden as the Holy of Holies, and Mount Sinai as the centre of the desert, a combinatiion that became important in later Christian speculation (Jub. 8:19). Josephus, *Jewish Wars*, III, 3.5, refers to Jerusalem as lying at the very centre of Judaea, "for which reason the town has sometimes, not inaptly, been called 'the navel of the country.'" The Sibylline Oracles V, 248–50, refer to "the godlike heavenly race of the blessed Jews, who dwell around the city of God at the centre of the earth."

Israel, then, is the centre of the earth; Jerusalem the centre of Israel; Mt. Zion the centre of Jerusalem; and, further, according to *BT* Sanhedrin 37a, the meeting place of the Sanhedrin lies within Mt. Zion and, again, within the Temple on its summit. The passage from *BT* Sanhedrin 37a reads:

The Gemara on Mishnah Sanhedrin 4:3,4 is as follows:

Whence is this derived? —R. Aha b. Hananiah [third century Amora] said: Scripture states, "Thy navel is like a round goblet" ['*aggân ha-Sahar*] wherein no mingled wine is wanting [Cant. vii, 3]. "Thy navel"—that is the Sanhedrin. Why was it called "*navel*"? Because it sat at the navel-point [i.e., the centre] of the world [compare *Tanḥuma, Wa Yikra*, xviii, 23].

And, finally, at the very centre of all the earth, stands the *'eben shetiyyah*, the foundation stone, which in the Second Temple occupied the place of the Holy Ark.

Such ideas had much influence on later Christian speculation, but for our specific purposes they are not of primary significance. They are widespread outside the Tanak in many cultures. In no way do they belong to the peculiarity of the biblical understanding of The Land. They belong mostly to the same category as the arrangement of the maps of the world that I knew as a boy. In these, the earth was not only largely coloured British red, but invariably had its centre in the British Isles, and, on closer inspection, in England, and, on still closer inspection, in London, until finally one detected Greenwich, by which the world set its clocks, but on which not even the sun itself would ever set. Nor are such ideas peculiarly British in the modern world. Readers of the very first page of Charles de Gaulle's *Memoirs of Hope* (translated 1971), will recall his understanding of his beloved France as "this human amalgam, on this territory, at the heart of this world." The very word *China* means centre of the universe.

Another notion of The Land, also not belonging to the peculiarity of the Tanak and Judaism, but important in its own right, is that of The Land of Israel as the place where Yahweh abundantly gave material gifts of all kinds to his people: it is this emphasis that makes so many passages in the Tanak useful in Harvest Thanksgiving services. We encounter here that element in Israel's thought on The Land which it probably owed primarily to Canaanite culture, but which it may have met before it settled in Canaan. Because primitive man was primarily concerned with the satisfaction of immediate physical needs, any area that offered such satisfaction became marked. On grounds of its fertility, usually because of the presence of a stream or spring or some other source of water, a certain spot would gain the reputation of being unique. Or, again, a peculiar conformation of rocks might create the belief that a place was in some way different. For whatever reason, a place would become associated with an irruption of the divine and come to be regarded as a gateway to a god. But because primitive man was a nomadic tribesman or huntsman, he could not conceive of the god as limited to one spot. The god surely moved within the area of man's seasonal migrations in search of water and grassland. And so the entire area which the god was considered to frequent became identified as his land, even though the first spot where he had manifested himself continued to be regarded as his home. Against such a picture, the patriarchal period has often been understood in terms of animism and the like, but few would now argue that the patriarch's religion is thus explicable.

The continued settlement in Canaan and the encounter with a static culture dominated by Baalim made the relationship (or the idea of such a relationship) between a god, as the giver of good gifts, and his land open to acute question. For the Canaanites, the god who guaranteed the fertility of the soil and the abundance of the harvest was Baal, "the husband" or "lord" of the land. The sanctuaries of the Baalim were usually situated in secluded, isolated spots near a source of water. The temptation for Israel to adopt them—sanctuaries and Baalim—was almost irresistible. During the battle waged by Israel against the Baalim in the interests of Yahweh, the functions of the Baalim were transferred to Yahweh, and it has been held that the reiterated emphases on the blessings of The Land came into Yahwehism through Canaanite Baalism. G. von Rad thinks that even the phrase "the land flowing with milk and honey" is from this source, as are the descriptions of an almost paradisal blessing on human progeny, on the offspring of the cattle, on basket and kneeding-trough, the fruit of the fields, rain for the earth, peace, deliverance from wild animals and so on; these descriptions would surely seem to have been composed under the influence of Canaanite nature-religion (Lev. 26:3–12; Num. 13:23, 28; 14:7 f.; 24:3 f.; Deut. 28:2–7).[1]

We may be allowed to question the exclusive ascription of such motifs to the influence of Canaanite religion without rejecting von Rad's main emphasis.

The question of the relationship of Yahweh to The Land of Israel cannot be isolated from the relationship of Yahweh to the whole universe. In the Tanak the notion of creation as a totality is late: the term *bârâ'*, to create, is not used of Yahweh before the Exile.[2] But certainly in the later strata of the Tanak Yahweh was always the creator, so it became wholly natural to regard him as the source of the gifts of the natural order entirely apart from his special relationship to Israel; the Canaanite heritage in this respect could easily be assimilated without any sense of incongruity.

These two peripheral aspects of The Land in the Tanak and Judaism—its centrality and abundance—do not, however, constitute its peculiarity. Before we pass on to that peculiarity, we might add a purely geographical factor which greatly affected Israel's understanding of its land: the difference between The Land of Israel, which received rain

1. G. von Rad, *The Problem of the Hexateuch and Other Essays*, p. 89.

2. On *bârâ'* see W. H. Bennett, *The Post-Exilic Prophets*, pp. 30 f. It might be objected that the exclusively postexilic appearance of *bârâ'* is not significant, because its equivalent, the verb *'sah*, occurs earlier. Nevertheless, the increasingly transcendent character of Yahweh after the Exile can hardly be gainsaid, as also the importance of the doctrine of creation in Judaism (see J. Bonsirven, *Le Judaïsme Palestinien*, I, 162 f.).

as proof of Yahweh's constant concern, and the land of Egypt, which was at the mercy of the fluctuations of the Nile. Israel was under Yahweh's immediate supervision in a way Egypt was not: the soil of Israel received water by the direct will and decision of Yahweh (Deut. 11:10–12). But few peoples have failed to discover some geographic sign of grace. The peculiarity about which we speak lies elsewhere, in the concepts of the Promised Land and of The Land as the peculiar property (*sᵉgûllâh*) of Yahweh.

THE LAND IN BIBLICAL SOURCES
The Hexateuch

First, The Land is a promised land. To disentangle the various currents that have gone into the concept of the promise of The Land is exceedingly difficult. Let us begin with those texts where the promise emerges in the oldest strata of the Pentateuch, which, it is generally agreed, occur in Gen. 15 [*EJ*]. In Gen. 15:1–6 we read as follows:

After these things the word of the Lord came to Abram in a vision, "Fear not, Abram, I am your shield; your reward shall be very great." But Abram said, "O Lord God, what wilt thou give me, for I continue childless, and the heir of my house is Eliezer of Damascus?" And Abram said, "Behold, thou hast given me no offspring; and a slave born in my house will be my heir." And behold, the word of the Lord came to him, "This man shall not be your heir." And he brought him outside and said, "Look toward heaven, and number the stars, if you are able to number them." Then he said to him, "So shall your descendants be." And he believed the Lord: and he reckoned it to him as righteousness.

Here Abraham is promised an heir. There is no explicit reference to land, but there is an implication in 15:4 that the land which Abraham possessed at that time was to be handed on to his son.

Later in the same chapter, in 15:17 ff. [*EJ*] we read:

When the sun had gone down and it was dark, behold, a smoking fire pot and a flaming torch passed between these pieces. On that day the Lord made a covenant with Abram, saying, "To your descendants I give this land [*'eretz*], from the river of Egypt to the great river, the river Euphrates, the land of the Kenites, the Kenizzites, the Kadmonites, the Hittites, the Perizzites, the Rephaim, the Amorites, the Canaanites, the Girgashites and the Jebusites."

The promise is referred to again in Gen. 12:1–3 [*J*] in the following terms:

Now the Lord said to Abram, "Go from your country [*'eretz*] and your kindred and your father's house to the land that I will show you. And I will make of you a great nation, and I will bless you, and make your name great, so that you will be a blessing. I will bless those who bless you, and him who curses you I will curse; and by you all the families of the earth shall bless themselves.

What is common to all these passages is that a land is promised to Abraham's descendants: the land they are to possess is to be theirs by divine authority. In other respects, the passages differ: in Gen. 15:17–21 the land defined is possibly, by implication, less extensive than that contemplated in Gen. 12:1–3, where Abraham's descendants are to become a great nation and to impinge upon all the families of the earth.

These passages have been variously assessed. According to some, they are creations of a late period, the Exile, when Israel felt that its possession of The Land was in jeopardy. She accordingly sought to bolster her claims by recourse to a supposedly ancient divine promise to Abraham. The promise is not grounded in early tradition, but is a late literary and theological construction, in this view, which has gained few adherents.

It has been urged that the promise is exceedingly ancient, going back to pre-Israelite and even pre-Canaanite times, when the god of Abraham, the god of a nomadic clan, promised to his devotees the two great needs of nomads—a land and numerous progeny. Later, when the descendants of this clan were incorporated into Israel, their god, the god of Abraham, later known as the God of the Fathers, was identified with Yahweh who had brought Israel out of Egypt. In this interpretation, the promise was given by the god of Abraham before Israel had entered Canaan: it envisaged not the gift of the whole Land of Palestine, but simply the strict inheritance of Abraham.

Recently, in the third place, the view has been forcefully presented that Abraham had already entered Canaan when the promise came to him. Of necessity, the god who gave the promise was not the god of a nomadic group, who had no land of his own to give, but the god of a settled community who owned the land which he gave in promise. The god concerned was, in fact, the *El* deity of Mamre at Hebron where Abraham dwelt. His name was possibly *El Shaddai*: the land he promised was the territory around Hebron referred to in Gen. 15:19 as the land of the Kenites, Kenizzites, and Kadmonites, etc. It is essential, in this view, to recognize that the patriarchs were not merely nomads but leaders of settlements in the agricultural land of Canaan. The emergence of the promise of The Land is to be understood as the legitimization of the settlement of the patriarchs in Canaan.

For the understanding of our task in this volume, what is important is not the rediscovery of the origins of the promise to Abraham, but the recognition that that promise was so reinterpreted from age to age that it became a living power in the life of the people of Israel. Not the mode of its origin matters, but its operation as a formative, dynamic, seminal force in the history of Israel. The legend of the promise entered so deeply into the experience of the

Jews that it acquired its own reality. What Jews believe to have happened in the Middle East has been no less formative in world history than that which is known to have occurred.

The reinterpretation to which we have referred concerned two things: the identity of the author of the promise and the content of the promise. As for the author of the promise, historically, if we follow Exod. 6:3, the god who gave the promise could not have been called Yahweh, because Yahweh was unknown by name to the patriarchs. Perhaps most scholars would agree that it is the Yahwist, that is, the formulator of what is known as the *J* tradition in the Pentateuch, who identified the original deity who had given the promise to Abraham with Yahweh. In this way it could be claimed that the god who gave the promise to Abraham also led Israel out of Egypt and became the God of Israel.

The history of the content of the promise is far more complicated. If we follow Clements,[3] it was governed by the political vicissitudes of the people of Judah and Israel and largely formulated by the Yahwist. In the original promise to Abraham, the content of the promise consists of progeny, blessing, and a land. In three passages, a new relationship to God is also promised. It is the promise of land alone that concerns us. The promise of the possession of the hereditary land of the clan or tribe, whether around Hebron or not, implied in Gen. 15:1 ff., was expanded to include the land from Egypt to the Euphrates (Gen. 15:18).

3. R. E. Clements, *Abraham and David*, pp. 47 ff. It is of the utmost significance that the borders of The Land were never precisely defined in the ancient sources, and that, like the early secular Zionists, even religious Jews have never in this century attempted to follow the broad biblical boundaries mechanically (see chapter 2, n. 26).

Further, Israel is to become a great nation, numerous as the stars of heaven in number (Gen. 15:5). Thus the promise is made to foretell the rise of the Davidic empire and subserve the interests of that empire. According to Clements, the covenant of Yahweh with David at his installation at Hebron (2 Kings 5:1 ff.) both reflects the Abrahamic covenant and influenced its interpretation and transmission. The Yahwist saw a connection between Abraham and David: for him the Abrahamic covenant found its fulfillment in the extension of the Davidic kingdom; the promise to Abraham was of the rise and triumph of that kingdom. The local dimension of the land in the promise originally made to Abraham was transcended. This means that the Abrahamic covenant became subsumed under the covenant with David, which in turn explains why there are so few references to Abraham and his covenant in the preexilic prophets and in the preexilic cultus.

As long as the Davidic dynasty prevailed, the appeal to the promise to Abraham, now absorbed into the Davidic covenant, could be neglected. But in times of dire crises, as in the eighth century, when the threat of Assyria was real, and the self-identity of the people was shaken, the Abrahamic covenant again gained recognition and importance. In Deuteronomy, although the covenant at Horeb is given preeminence, appeal is also made to the promise to Abraham, in reassurance that behind Israel's existence and its tenure of the land of Canaan lay the divine purpose. The Abrahamic covenant is now referred to as having been made with all the three patriarchs and is understood as exclusively concerned with the land of Canaan. The land promised to Abraham has been promised to Israel as a whole, and the promise has found its fulfillment, both in the covenant at Horeb and in the conquest under Joshua.

Deuteronomy, then, fused together the promise of The Land made to the early patriarchs and the tradition of the giving of the Law at Sinai. The relationship of the commandments to The Land is regarded in Deuteronomy as twofold. On the one hand, the commandments are regulatory; that is, they are intended to provide guidance for the government of The Land, for the conduct of the cultus, and for the arrangements demanded by the settlement. On the other hand, the commandments are conditional; that is, only if they are observed can The Land received because of the promise to the Fathers be possessed. According to Deuteronomy, under the terms of the covenant entered into at Sinai, Israel, if it disobeys the commandments, can be expelled from The Land: in this sense, the occupancy of The Land has a "legal" basis. Yes: but Deuteronomy finds reassurance for Israel in the promise to Abraham. That promise was irrevocable: it can, therefore, provide a rationale for forgiveness, even though the commandments have been broken. In this way, the promise to Abraham gives grounds for ultimate hope. In Deuteronomy the covenant of "grace" with Abraham can be read as a guarantee and safeguard against failure to observe the covenant of "the Law"—even as a "gospel" for Israel. Particularly revealing of this are the words of Moses to the people in Deut. 9:24–29.

When later we come to *P*, the priestly document, the strict historical origins and limits of the promise to Abraham are still further modified. The priestly document seeks to provide Israel with a renewed theological basis for its existence. Taking up *J* and *E*, *P* makes the divine promise to Abraham the bedrock on which all Israel's subsequent history rests. *P*'s understanding of that covenant is seen in Gen. 17:1–14 [*P*]:

When Abram was ninety-nine years old the Lord appeared to Abram, and said to him, "I am God Almighty; walk before me, and be blameless. And I will make my covenant between me and you, and will multiply you exceedingly." Then Abram fell on his face; and God said to him, "Behold, my covenant is with you, and you shall be the father of a multitude of nations. I will make you exceedingly fruitful; and I will make nations of you, and kings shall come forth from you. And I will establish my covenant between me and you and your descendants after you throughout their generations for an everlasting covenant, to be God to you and to your descendants after you. And I will give to you, and to your descendants after you, the land ['eretz] of your sojournings, all the land ['eretz] of Canaan, for an everlasting possession; and I will be their God."

And God said to Abraham, "As for you, you shall keep my covenant, you and your descendants after you throughout their generations. This is my covenant, which you shall keep, between me and your descendants after you: Every male among you shall be circumcised. You shall be circumcised in the flesh of your foreskins, and it shall be a sign of the covenant between me and you. He that is eight days old among you shall be circumcised; every male throughout your generations, whether born in your house, or bought with your money from any foreigner who is not of your offspring, both he that is born in your house and he that is bought with your money, shall be circumcised. So shall my covenant be in your flesh an everlasting covenant. Any uncircumcised male who is not circumcised in the flesh of his foreskin shall be cut off from his people; he has broken my covenant."

Here Abraham is to be the father of a multitude of nations; all the land of Canaan is to be an everlasting possession; the god of the Abrahamic covenant (*El Shaddai* was probably his name historically) is to be the god of Abraham's descendants; and circumcision is to be the mark of god's people. The content of the covenant has thus been changed: its promissory character has been heightened; its inviolability has been affirmed—it is everlasting. *P* exhibits what is already found in Deuteronomy—an appeal to divine grace, the promise, as a bulwark against failure to observe the commandments of the Sinai covenant, which *P*, like Deuteronomy, connects with the Abrahamic covenant. The appeal to the Abrahamic covenant means that Israel's election, and with it the possession of The Land, can never, for *P*, become conditional on obedience to the Law; that election, resting upon the Abrahamic covenant, cannot be annulled by human disobedience. Israel, it follows, cannot be destroyed, and The Land *will* be hers.

According to von Rad, the whole of the Hexateuch in all its vast complexity was governed by the theme of the fulfillment of the promise to Abraham in the settlement in Canaan. "The chief purpose of this work," he wrote, "was to present in all its biblical and theological significance this one leading conception, in relation to which all the other conceptions of the Hexateuch assume an ancillary role."[4] Like Clements, von Rad holds that it was the work of the Yahwist to fuse the whole complex of the patriarchal sagas together: for him, the entry into Palestine under Joshua is the fulfillment of the promise. Later modifications of this basic pattern of *J* and *E*, in von Rad's view, were trivial.

Of all the promises made to the patriarchs, it was that of The Land that was most prominent and decisive. It is the linking together of the promise to the patriarchs *with* the fulfillment of it in the settlement that gives to the Hexateuch its distinctive theological character. For the Hexateuch, The Land is a promised land, and that inviolably. The significance of the promise as a fact in the Hexateuch is immeasurable, for a very simple reason. However much the Prophets and the Writings gained in significance, in

4. Von Rad, *Problem of the Hexateuch,* pp. 85 ff.

later ages the Pentateuch remained the bedrock of revelation for Jews, so that the references to the promise of The
Land embedded in it must be accorded great weight in any
assessment of Judaism.[5]

5. In *Torah and Canon*, J. A. Sanders has concentrated on the
distinction between the Hexateuch and the Pentateuch. He asks
the simple question why the Pentateuch, not the Hexateuch, came
to constitute the heart of the Torah for Judaism. The "story," the
memory of which alone kept "Israel" alive, in *J* and *E* (composed
or collected between the eleventh and eighth centuries B.C.E.)
included the conquest of the land, and stretched on to include the
monarchy of David. Sanders has pointed out in an unpublished
paper that the conquest of Canaan in the book of Joshua
"culminated in the very place where Abraham first settled, at
Shechem: the promise of the land, which was made to Abraham
at Shechem, was symbolically fulfilled at Shechem." Would it not
have been natural for Judaism to elevate the Hexateuch to a normative position? Apparently so. Yet it was Deuteronomy, a document from the seventh century which leaves Moses looking to
the Promised Land but not entering it, that formed the climax of
the Torah of Judaism. Why? Sanders answers that the crisis of the
sixth century B.C.E., in which The Land, the city, and the Temple
were lost and ceased to sustain "Israel," compelled the Deu-
teronomist, and later *P* (sixth–fifth centuries B.C.E.), to look back
to the period before the conquest, the Mosaic age, as that which
supplied an authoritative norm, and to which both *D* and *P*
ascribed the laws which were to give life. While this deserves
serious examination, we would simply ask whether Sanders has
not too rigidly separated *torah* as "law" from *torah* as "story," and
whether, although Judaism did elevate the Pentateuch, it did not
isolate it.

The story of the "conquest" in the book of Joshua still remains
part of the Tanak. (Cf., especially, D. N. Freedman's review of
GL, and B. S. Childs, *Introduction to the Old Testament as
Scripture*, pp. 56–57.) If Sanders should be able to establish his
case, it would be difficult to account for the persistence of the
territorial doctrine with which we are here concerned. His work
suggests at least that there was much flexibility in the attitude to

This notion, that The Land belongs to Yahweh himself, persisted throughout the Tanak, and beyond. It expressed itself in the conviction that the soil of Israel was not tribal property, but was given by Yahweh for cultivation by lot: the individual received his parcel of land by lot, and so, too, did the tribe. The whole Land was divided according to lot (Num. 26:55). Judgment rendered by lot was thought to be that of Yahweh himself. Thus, when Yahweh commanded that The Land be divided according to lot, it was he himself who decided upon its division: because The Land was Yahweh's alone, he alone could decide its allocation (Ezek, 47:13 f.).

Cultic statements about the harvest are to be understood in the light of Yahweh's ownership of The Land. This explains the demand for the offering of firstlings; of the first son in Exod. 22:28; the tithe given to the Levites in Lev. 18:24; the tithe of all the yield of the seed in Deut. 14:22; and of all the produce in Deut. 26:9–15. In the Hebraic mind, the first of a particular series was the archetypal form, and as such represented the entire species. Thus, the offering of the firstfruits symbolized the offering of the entire crop or harvest. Since Yahweh was the owner of The Land, the firstfruits offering was only a rendering to him of his proper portion. For as The Land belonged to Yahweh so, rightfully, did all the produce. The same concept governed the custom of gleaning.

Yahweh's possession of The Land is further acknowledged in the commandment that The Land should keep a sabbath to the Lord (Lev. 25:2, 4). The sabbath of The Land has been variously explained, but Lev. 25:2 reads: ". . . the land shall keep a sabbath to the Lord." It is not the people who are commanded to allow The Land to rest: rather The Land itself, personified, seems to be addressed. The Land, too, owes worship to Yahweh, to signify that special relationship which it enjoys with him. The Land's rest recalls the seventh-day rest of the Lord himself after the creation.

Yahweh's possession of The Land was expressed in terms of "holiness," a conception which in its origin had little, if anything, to do with morality, but rather denoted a relationship of separation for, or consecration to, a god. Since The Land was Yahweh's possession, it enjoyed a certain degree of closeness to him; for Yahweh dwelt in the midst of Israel (Num. 25:34). Because Yahweh was near to it, his own holiness radiated throughout its boundaries. Note that the term "holy land," which suggests that The Land itself was inherently "holy," seldom occurs in the Tanak; that is, the holiness of The Land is entirely derivative.

Nevertheless, the potency of the concept of the holiness of The Land, though only derived from its relationship to Yahweh, emerges particularly in passages which forcibly and vividly personify The Land. Consider especially Lev. 20:22–26 (*H: P*). Here The Land is conceived of as itself ejecting Israelites when they are unfaithful to the commandments. One might conclude from this that it was the transgression of the specifically Israelite Law, the Torah, that provoked The Land and caused it to react violently. But in Lev. 18:24–30, The Land had been defiled by its pre-Israelite inhabitants, who did not know the Torah of Moses, but had broken the demands that The Land itself imposed. It was not the military prowess of the Israelites, nor even Yahweh's fighting for them, which had caused the expulsion of the earlier inhabitants of The Land. When it became defiled by their abominations, The Land itself thrust them out. The implication is that it was already holy in Canaanite days, because Yahweh owned it and dwelt in the midst of it. This is the import of Num. 25:34: "You shall not defile the land in which you live, in the midst of which I dwell, for I the Lord dwell in the midst of the people of Israel."

The relationship of The Land to Yahweh also governed the relationship of the Law to The Land. If the Israelites were to live in Yahweh's Land, in his very presence, they had to approximate to his holiness by following his Law: the verse "You shall be holy; for I the Lord your God am holy" (Lev. 19:1) implies that Israel is to obey Yahweh's Law. And, in much of the Tanak, obedience to the Law becomes the condition of occupying The Land, as we have already seen. We shall return to this theme later. Suffice it here to refer to Isa. 1:19 and Deut. 4:40. Here it is important to recognize that Yahweh had imposed on The Land—indeed upon nature—a sacred order or pattern or law, the violation of which produced a dissolution, a return to chaotic disorder and formlessness. This can best be illustrated from those laws which, when disobeyed, are specifically stated to pollute or defile The Land of Israel. We note prohibitions:

1. Against harlotry (Lev. 19:29)
2. Against shedding blood (Num. 29–34; Deut. 21:6–9; Ps. 106:38 f.)
3. Against allowing a corpse to remain hanging on a tree (Deut. 21:22–23)
4. Against remarriage with a former divorced and remarried wife (Deut. 24:1–4; compare Jer. 3:1)

To examine the background of these prohibitions in full is not possible here. Fundamental is the concept of totality within the Israelite community. Everything within that community had its proper place: everything in the natural order was divided according to function or kind. For example, there could be no violation of species, no crossing of the boundaries set between differing groups. This explains the prohibitions expressed in Lev. 19:19; 22:5, 9, 10, 11. There is a Yahweh-given order to the cosmos; a division is made between the sacred and the profane (Lev. 22:5 ff.).

And it can safely be asserted that each of the prohibitions singled out here is directed against the violation of that order and the mixing of the sacred and profane which leads to the disintegration and profanation of the whole cosmos. Thus prostitution violated the concept of totality. The prostitute withdrew from the community as an integrated whole: by dissolving the boundaries between kinds, she violated the sacred divisions established by Yahweh. Again, blood was especially holy to Semites: blood was life: it was the possession of Yahweh as his portion of a sacrificial feast, and as such was sacred. To shed blood was to handle what was sacred as though it were profane. So, too, because dead bodies were one of the major sources of uncleanness, to allow a corpse to lie in The Land, and especially to hang it on a tree overnight was to subject The Land, which in virtue of its relation to Yahweh was holy, to uncleanness. From the corpse, uncleanness spread like a contagion throughout the surrounding area: the totality of nature was thereby affected. And, finally, the prohibition against remarrying one's divorced wife who had remarried was governed by the recognition that such a woman was in a similar case to the prostitute: she had known two different men. To return to her first husband was to mix diverse kinds and ipso facto to join together one who was clean (the first husband) with the one who had, by her second marriage, become unclean. Again, such a violation of the natural order involved the whole cosmos, and was particularly manifested in The Land itself.

But it is merely for the sake of clarity that we have concentrated on the above four prohibitions. What is true of them holds true of every violation of Yahweh's commandments. Yahweh dwells in Israel. Through the contagion of his holiness, The Land becomes clean. Violation of Yahweh's Law is a profanation of the order which he has implanted in the cosmos. And when, through the violation of that Law, Israelites have profaned themselves, they can no longer remain in the holy-clean Land; either The Land itself ejects them, as in some passages, or The Land suffers under the wrath which they have brought upon it, in which case, as Is. 24:4–5 puts the matter:

The earth mourns and withers, the world languishes and withers; the heavens languish together with the earth. The earth lies polluted under its inhabitants: for they have transgressed the laws, violated the statutes, broken the everlasting covenant.

In the above pages, we have distinguished two peculiar emphases in the understanding of The Land in the Tanak. The first is an historical one, centered on the promise to Abraham and appearing chiefly in the narrative portions of the Hexateuch, in *J* and *E*. The second is a cultic one, concentrating on the conception of The Land as Yahweh's own possession and appearing chiefly in the legislative portions of the Hexateuch, *D* and *P*. Although derived from different sources, these two emphases became merged in the cultic life of Israel and in its transmission of various traditional documents, so that, as the Tanak now stands, they have to be carefully disentangled. Proper assessment of the role they played throughout the history of Israel is difficult, and will be postponed for the present.

The Prophets: Doom and Restoration

The second source to which we turn is the prophetic literature. One thing seems clear: concern with The Land and hope for The Land emerges at many places in the Tanak outside the Hexateuch. While the promise was regarded as fulfilled in the settlement, that settlement was not regarded as a complete fulfillment. Deuteronomy makes it clear that there is still a future to look forward to: The Land has to achieve rest and peace. This points to what von Rad calls one of the most interesting problems of Tanak theology. He expresses it thus: "Promises which have been fulfilled in history are not thereby exhausted of their content, but remain as promises on a different level, although they are to some extent metamorphosed in the process. The promise of the land was proclaimed ever anew, even after its fulfillment, as a future benefit of God's redemptive activity."[7] Promise and fulfillment inform much of the Tanak, and the tradition, however changed, continued to embody the hope of life in The Land.

Thus it is arguable that it was as inconceivable to the prophets as to the people as a whole that Israel should finally be deprived of her Land. At this point, we encounter a notorious problem of proportion in the interpretation of the prophets. It has been easy and, indeed, almost customary, to assert that the prophetic sources suggest something along the following lines: the prophets insisted on Yahweh's freedom to choose and to reject Israel from the beginning, but they recognized that Israel as a whole had been unfaithful to her covenant with him, and maintained that Yahweh could exist without his people—that, indeed, it might become his will to destroy them. The prophets pronounced doom on people and Land: it is this predominant message of doom that rings like a knell in their works. And it has been pointed out that one, at least, of the greatest of the prophets seems to have been able to feel only a loose commitment to The Land, deep as was his love for it. The advice of Jeremiah in a letter to the exiles in Babylon reveals

7. Ibid., pp. 92 f.

this (Jer. 29:1, 4–9). In the popular mind, return from Babylon was an absolute necessity; for Jeremiah it was no urgent matter, although he was hopeful that someday it would occur: for the moment, to return to The Land would be to follow false prophecy.

But it is not only in 29:1, 4–9 that Jeremiah takes a positive view of the Exile. Jeremiah 29:16–20 and 38:2 make clear that those who were not deported, but remained in The Land and in the city of Jerusalem, would know the sword and famine and pestilence. The words of Jer. 38:2 are unequivocal: "Thus saith the Lord, He who stays in this city shall die by the sword, by famine and by pestilence; but he who goes out to the Chaldeans shall live; he shall have his life as a prize of war, and live." Equally striking is the vision of the good and bad figs in Jer. 24:1–30. The good figs are the exiles (Jer. 24:5). The evil figs are those who remain in The Land (Jer. 24:8–9). For Jeremiah, the Exile is the fulfillment of the purpose of God: the exiles are blessed in their disaster. The same theology reemerges in Ezek. 17 in the parable of the eagle and the cedar. As in Jeremiah, the Exile proves a blessing.

But no other prophet so unequivocally asserts the possiblity of the good life apart from The Land and we may well question whether the attitude of Jeremiah and Ezekiel was as unclouded as we have suggested. As the prophetic books now stand, alongside prophecies of doom against The Land because of Israel's sin, there are promises of restoration. This is particularly conspicuous in Amos (9:14–15). Compare also the incidence of prophecies of restoration in Hos. 1:10; Is. 2:1–5; 9:1–9 (both possibly Isaianic); 9:10–16; 24–27; 26:15–20; 29:16–21; 32:15–20; Jer. 3:18–19; 11:4–5; and Ezek. 4:15. Many such messages of restoration in the prophetic sources, as they now stand, are doubtless due to emendation aimed at the domestication of the prophets.

Like the generality in Israel, stung by prophetic denunciation and foreboding, pious scribes could not reconcile themselves to the severity of the prophets, and provided addenda to soften their implacable stance. To such scribes, the prophets' messages of doom could not possibly have been their last word. The question, however, is whether *all* the prophecies of restoration to The Land are to be so understood.

If we exclude Amos and Isaiah, all the prophets of doom reveal a persistent yearning for the ingathering of the dispersed of Israel into one national entity in their own Land. At first sight, there is nothing in Amos to suggest the recognition of a peculiar relationship between Israel and her Land. Amos 7:17 is instinct with awareness of the significance of The Land, however, and there may be a glimmer of hope for people in The Land expressed in 5:14, notwithstanding that the closing words of Amos 9:11–15, speaking of a coming salvation, cannot with certainty be derived from the prophet. It is significant that Israel's punishment for her sins takes the two forms, among others, of a redistribution of The Land and exile from it (7:17; compare 5:26). Future restoration of the people and its Land can only be very tentatively found, if at all, in Amos.

It is otherwise when we turn to Hosea. The words of hope in Hos. 1:10–11 can only very doubtfully be ascribed to the prophet, but those of 2:14–25 may be taken as his. Here Yahweh is to entice his unfaithful Israel (2:2–15) back to himself in the wilderness. But notice: it is not in the wilderness that Israel is to enjoy new fertility, but as she reenters the promised Land, through the Valley of Achor, where Achan sinned (Josh. 7:24 ff.). This has now become a door of hope. Unlike the Rechabites, whom we shall mention later, the prophet does not wish a return to the desert: such a return as is envisaged in 2:2–14 is merely a prelude to a new entry into the land. And that land is Yahweh's Land. That the land of Canaan is The Land of the Lord appears in 9:3. The attitude towards The Land in Hosea is a positive one: despite its apostasy, Israel is to dwell in The Land.

The role of The Land in Isaiah is less easy to assess. But one thing is clear: that the reward of sin is thought of in terms of The Land indicates its significance (see Isa. 24). There is no doubt that The Land is the Land of Emmanuel (Isa. 8:8; cf. 14:25). The seminal passage is 1:5–9 (compare Isa. 5:13, where exile is the punishment for sin, 7:23–4; and 9:19). Beyond the destruction of The Land, Isaiah looks forward to a renewal of Zion and the perpetuation of a remnant of the people. True, unlike Hosea, he makes no reference to an exile and a return, but he does look forward to a new king and his kingdom (Isa. 9:7). Here The Land is not explicitly mentioned, but the kingdom of the new David implies the restored Land—restored in justice and righteousness, not in its old sinful form.

When we turn to Jeremiah, the evidence leads to the same attitude. Born in Anathoth, which is situated in the territory of Benjamin, it was perhaps natural that Jeremiah should have been concerned not merely with his own kingdom of Judah but also with the fate of the northern kingdom exiled in 722 B.C.E., because Benjamin (although politically it was possessed by both north and south at different times) ethnologically belonged to Israel. At any rate, his prophecies reveal an absorbing interest and a constant love for the Rachel tribes; it is his heart's desire that the northern Israel as well as Judah should ultimately return from exile. Here we must emphasize his purchase of a portion of his family inheritance: this is symbolic of his belief in the ultimate salvation of all his people and their establishment upon their own soil (Jer. 32:6–25). If we take

Jer. 31:2–6, 18–26 as authentic and accept the literal interpretation of them that Skinner favours, they reveal the
same longing. This means that for Jeremiah the nation was
still the sphere, if not the unit, of religion. As Skinner puts
it: "The main point is that in some sense a restoration of the
Israelite nationality was the form in which Jeremiah conceived the Kingdom of God." It is essential to note in the
vision of the figs in Jer. 24 that the "good figs," the exiles,
will be brought again to The Land (Jer. 24:6) (compare Jer.
12:14b–15; 16:15; 24:6; 29:14; 30:3; 31:9, 12, 14, 23–25,
33–34).

In Ezekiel we find the idea that Yahweh is a jealous god
who can brook no rivals. He therefore inflicts punishment
on Israel because of her apostasy, but the restoration of
Israel is assured, because Yahweh's name must be upheld
among the nations; the failure of his people would bring
dishonour upon himself. The ingathering of all scattered
Israelites in The Land is a constant theme of Ezekiel; the
reassembled nation will be purified in heart and spirit; there
will be one flock under the shepherd Yahweh (Ezek. 17;
compare Ezek. 20:42; 36:9–12; 39:26). (The end of Ezek.
47:15–48:35 describes the redistribution of The Land
among the tribes of Israel.)

The same motif runs through Deutero-Isaiah. True, Israel is to be a missionary to the Gentiles, but its first task,
before turning to them, is to seek the return of the lost
sheep of the house of Israel (Is. 49:5 f.). There is a core of
particularism in the most universal of the prophets.

That the hope for the future in the prophets' messages is
not to be neglected is confirmed by recent studies. It is
preserved even when the promise seems obliterated in the
announcement of doom. The "Day" of Yahweh, which
spelt judgment, would also witness the outpouring of his
mercy. This hope comes to explicit expression in much-

noticed concepts: that of the remnant in Isaiah, that of the new covenant in Jeremiah, and that of the spirit revivifying the dry bones in Ezekiel. These concepts have been treated so often that we need merely pinpoint the pertinent aspects. The remnant which is envisaged, not only by Isaiah but also by Amos, assures not only survival but continuity with the old community, and it exists not for its own sake, but for the sake of the whole community: within the perspective of Israel itself, it is *always* a saving remnant. Likewise, although the new covenant of Jeremiah suggests a radically new beginning, it is with Israel, albeit a changed people, that this new covenant is to be ratified; just as it is the people of Israel which is to be reconstituted when, in Ezekiel's vision, the spirit revivifies the dry bones. It may be objected that neither the remnant nor the new covenant nor the spirit specifically refer to The Land. But this may be questioned in the case of Isa. 7:3, where clearly the remnant (*She 'ar yâshûb*) is involved in the very physical existence of the nation. In any case, in view of the passages we have cited in this connection, the prophets did include The Land in their hopes for the future. Despite the difficulty of their precise delimitation, if we bear in mind the passages promising restoration in the prophets, together with references to the remnant, the new covenant, and the spirit, it is difficult not to recognize with Sifre[8] that the prophets first addressed hard words of judgment to Israel, but in the end spoke words of consolation.

8. Cited without exact reference in *New Light from the Prophets*, p. 14, by L. Finkelstein, who translates: "And 'all' the Prophets learned from him [Moses], at first addressing harsh words to Israel, but in the end turning about and speaking words of consolation." Finkelstein notes, as examples, Hosea, Joel, Amos, Micah, and Jeremiah.

Finkelstein, in a controversial work[9], has connected the prophets with the legal tradition that came *after* them, that is, with the development of the rabbinic tradition (just as Alt, Buber, von Rad, Zimmerli, and others have connected the prophets with the Law in Israel *before* their day). If his interpretation is accepted the concern of the prophets with, and their anticipation of, the future life of their people in The Land becomes exceedingly probable, however dark the doom they proclaimed. In Finkelstein's hands, the prophets become, to use Rudolf Otto's phrase, architects of the future, as well as heralds of destruction: they reveal the essential irrationality of the eschatological mind, which can hold doom and a promising future in living tension.[10]

THE LAND IN EXTRABIBLICAL SOURCES
The Apocrypha and Pseudepigrapha

After the last of the canonical prophets, hope for The Land is taken over into later eschatological thinking in Israel. The problem of how far Apocalyptic is an outgrowth of prophecy or is a new emergence primarily instigated by the influence of Iranian and other factors on the life of Israel need not directly concern us. What does need recognition is that eschatological thinking was not alien to the main currents in Judaism. The antithesis drawn between Pharisaism as the heir of the Law and Apocalyptic as the heir of prophecy—so that, with the increasing significance of Pharisaism, Apocalyptic became correspondingly peripheral in Judaism—has had to be abandoned. This means that concepts that appear in the apocalyptic sources need not be regarded as insignificant fringe elements in Judaism. In these sources, The Land is given the kind of attention that

9. Ibid.
10. R. Otto, *The Kingdom of God and the Son of Man*, pp. 59 ff.

is accorded to it in the Tanak and in the rabbinical sources, although notably less frequently.

The incidence of specific references to The Land in the Apocrypha, the Pseudepigrapha, and the Qumran scrolls, especially in comparison with the Hexateuch, is meagre. But the awareness of The Land—its holiness, its possible pollution by sin, and consequent need for purification—is unmistakably clear. The connection of Israel with The Land is an assumption. The term "holy land" appears (Wisd. Sol. 13:3, 4, 7; 2 Bar. 65:9, 10; 71:1; Sib. Or. 3:266 f.), and "goodly land" (Tob. 14:4, 5; Jub. 13:2, 6; 1 En. 89:40), and "the land which is in thy sight the most precious of all lands" (Wisd. Sol. 13:3, 4, 7). In 1 En. 89:40, the phrase "pleasant and glorious land" occurs, and in the Letter of Aristeas, line 107, The Land is "extensive and beautiful." The notion of The Land of promise occurs in Jub. 12:22; 13:3; 22:27; Ecclus. 46:8; Asmp. M. 1:8 f.; 2:1. The connection between Israel's conduct and The Land is marked. In Jub. 6:12–13, failure to observe the demands of Yahweh is incompatible with occupation of The Land. Again, in Jub. 15:28, the reward of those who observe circumcision is that "they will *not* be rooted out of the land." The cultic recital of Yahweh's acts in history was the vehicle for the transmission and perpetuation of the understanding of the relationship between people and land, as of other motifs. Even the rationalization of the conquest as a punishment for the sins of the pre-Israelite inhabitants reappears in the Wisdom of Solomon (cf. 2:7). The insistence on the mercifulness of Yahweh, even in the conquest, however, breaks through in 12:3–11.

The understanding of The Land found in the Tanak, then, reappears in the Apocrypha and Pseudepigrapha, showing the growth in intensity of the idea that Yahweh must vindicate his choice of his people by restoring them to

their land according to their tribes as a united people. Perhaps the most well-known expression of this idea is found
in Psalms of Solomon (first century B.C.E.). Speaking of
the son of David, whom the Lord shall raise up, the author
writes:

> And he shall gather together a holy people. . . .
> And he shall divide them according to their
> tribes upon the land
> And neither sojourner nor alien shall
> sojourn with them any more.

In 4 Ezra 13:48 (first century C.E.) we read of the last
days that: "The survivors of thy people, even those found
within thy holy border (shall be saved)." The same thought
occurs in 2 Bar. 9:2 (first century C.E.). In the end, Yahweh
will protect only the people who live in Israel: that land will
be surrounded by his holy presence:

For at that time I will protect only those who are found in those
self-same days in this land.

In 71:1 the author asserts that The Land itself will act on
behalf of Israel:

And the holy land shall have mercy on its own and it shall protect
its inhabitants at that time.

Only by such protection as God and The Land itself provide will the name of Israel be remembered. As 2 Bar.
3:4–5 expresses it:

What, therefore, will there be for these things [that is, at the end]?
for if thou destroyest thy city and deliverest up thy land to those
who hate us, how shall the name of Israel be remembered?

In concurrence with the "active" role ascribed to The Land
itself in 2 Bar., in 4 Ezra The Land becomes "holy" or

sanctified in the last days because Yahweh draws especially near to it. The Israelites will escape from the dangers and terrors of the end through no merit of their own. Their only guarantee of salvation will lie in their actually dwelling in The Land, which Yahweh will save for his own sake alone, as his own possession. 4 Ezra 9:7–9 makes this clear:

And everyone shall survive from the perils aforesaid and shall see salvation in my land, and within my borders which I have sanctified for myself eternally.

Even in 1 Enoch (first century C.E.?), at 90:20, cosmic and supraterrestrial as are its visions of the future, at the end it is in the pleasant Land of Israel that the throne of Yahweh is finally to be erected.

The Qumran Writings

The high evaluation and significance of The Land is also present in the documents from Qumran. In these The Land is understood as Yahweh's own possession. In *IQS* 1:5, we read that the members of the sect are "to practice truth and righteousness and justice *in the land*." The council of the community is characterized as follows in *IQS* 8:3:

In the council of the community (there shall be) twelve laymen and three priests who are perfect in all that is revealed of the whole Torah, through practicing truth and righteousness and justice and loving devotion and walking humbly each with his fellow *in order to maintain faithfulness in the land* with a steadfast intent and with a broken Spirit [emphasis added].

Further in *IQS* 8:4b–7 we read:

When these things come to pass in Israel, the Council of the Community will have been established in truth:
As an eternal planting, a holy house for Israel,
A most holy institution for Aaron,
Witnesses of truth concerning judgment,

And the chosen of grace to atone for the land
And to render to the wicked their desert [emphasis added].

The council of the community is to be "accepted to make atonement for the land" (*IQS* 8:10). The life of the community, in accordance with its own understanding of the Law, is designed to achieve what the sacrificial system had in vain sought to accomplish, the acceptance of The Land by Yahweh. *IQS* 9:3 ff. reads:

When these things come to pass in Israel according to all these regulations, for a foundation of a holy spirit, for eternal truth, *for a ransom for the guilt of transgression and sinful faithlessness, and for acceptance for the land* [emphasis added].

Part of the purpose of the community is to restore a land made unclean to acceptance. There is an "order" of The Land which the Law recognizes and which is to be observed in human habitations (*CDC* 9:6b). The tribal organization of The Land is assumed (*IQM* 2): even in war, the Jubilee of The Land is to be honoured (*IQM* 2). The relationship between human conduct and The Land, which we so often discover in the Tanak, is assumed throughout the scrolls. Sin leads Yahweh to hide his face from The Land (*CDC* 2:9–11) and causes The Land to become desolate (*CDC* 4:10). One significant mark of sin is the removal of the boundaries of The Land, which, as we have seen, were regarded as set by Yahweh himself (*CDC* 1:16; 8:1). But, however deep the consciousness of the corruption of The Land through sin, it is of the very genius of the Qumran community that it recognizes that the condition of The Land is not totally hopeless, because a "remnant"— the sect itself—has been spared to atone for it. The awareness of the peculiarity of Israel, and its stance against other lands, is clear: Israel stands against the nations. In the last days, warriors from its tribes are to go out against the Gentile

lands (*IQM* 2). For the author, at the time of the return of
the exiles from the desert of the peoples (col. 1:3, compare
Ezek. 20:35), the sect, the true Israelites, would occupy The
Land, according to their tribes, and institute an offensive
war against those outside. With The Land as its base, this
was to be a holy war, much more intense and widespread
than those conceived in the Tanak, which were usually
defensive. What concerns us here is the centrality of The
Land of Israel in the thought of the author, in line with Isa.
2:1–5 and especially Ezek. 38 ff.

Our brief survey of the Apocrypha, Pseudepigrapha, and
Qumran writings reflects the comparative infrequency of
references to The Land in these sources. This must, however, be qualified. After the Exile, the sentiment concerning The Land became concentrated in Jerusalem and the
Temple, references to which in the sources used are very
numerous. The absence of direct references to The Land
can, therefore, be misleading, because The Land is implied
in the city and the Temple, which became its quintessence.
(See, e.g., Tob. 13:13, 17; and especially 14:5, which looks
forward to a future Temple to which the exiles will return
as to a rebuilt house; at the same time, 14:7 claims that all
the children of Israel shall dwell forever in The Land of
Abraham in safety, and it shall be given over to them.)
Moreover, brief as it is, our treatment has brought into
focus two factors. First, the difference between the approach to The Land in the Apocrypha and Pseudepigrapha
and that in the Qumran writings, which we shall enlarge
upon and seek to explain below, and, secondly, the relationship between historical events and the approach to
The Land. We saw in dealing with the Hexateuch how *D*
and *P* reacted to the collapse of the state in the sixth century
B.C.E. The same reaction is traceable mutatis mutandis in 2
Bar. and 4 Ezra where, after C.E. 70, there emerges an

almost desperate concentration on the efficacy of life in The Land. Indeed, these documents seem to go further than *D* and *P*. There are passages in the Tanak where The Land expels unworthy inhabitants: in 2 Bar. and 4 Ezra, as we have seen it acts, not only negatively, but positively on behalf of "Israel." Such a note could only emerge out of desperation, which was probably more typical of apocalyptic circles than of the rabbinic ones, to which we turn next.

The Rabbinic Sources

In many apocalyptic and "sectarian" groups, then, the question of The Land remained a living issue up to the first century. Such groups, as we saw above, have often been claimed to be outside the dominant Pharisaic stream of Judaism, so that their concern with The Land might be discounted by some as a mark of insignificant currents. But such an approach to first-century Judaism is no longer possible. The customary picture of first-century Judaism before C.E. 70 as dominated by the Pharisees, who constituted the representatives of what has been called normative Judaism, is not tenable: differences of emphasis there were between apocalyptists and Pharisees, but no cleavage. We shall find that, on the question of The Land, the Pharisees largely shared the views of the groups referred to.

In fact, Pharisaism so cherished the view that there was an unseverable connection between Israel and Yahweh and The Land, that this view has been especially connected with the devastation of The Land by the Romans in the war of C.E. 66–70. Conditions in Palestine after C.E. 70 were economically difficult. As a result, there developed an increasing tendency for Jews to emigrate from Palestine to neighbouring countries, especially to Syria. This became so serious that it threatened to depopulate The Land. The need to encourage Jews to remain in it was so urgent that the Pharisaic leaders after C.E. 70 adopted a policy of extolling the virtues of The Land and encouraging settlement. Conservative sages, such as Rabbi Eliezer the Great or ben Hyrcanus (C.E. 80–120), in order to protect Palestinian agriculture wanted to subject Syrian agriculture to all the requirements of tithing and the sabbatical year so as to check the emigration of farmers to Syria. R. Gamaliel II (C.E. 80–120), while he opposed such extreme measures, also shared in this purpose. The following passage from Mishnah Hallah iv: 7–8 is instructive:

7. If Israelites leased a field from gentiles in Syria, R. Eliezer declares their produce liable to tithes and subject to the Seventh Year law; but Rabban Gamaliel declares it exempt. Rabban Gamaliel says: Two Dough-offerings [are given] in Syria. But R. Eliezer says: One Dough-offering. [Beforetime] they accepted the more lenient ruling of Rabban Gamaliel and the more lenient ruling of R. Eliezer, but afterward they followed the rulings of Rabban Gamaliel in both things.

8. Rabban Gamaliel says: Three regions are distinguished in what concerns Dough-offering. In the land of Israel as far as Chezib one Dough-offering [is given]: from Chezib to the River [Eastward; to the Euphrates] and to Amanah, [Northward, to the river Amanah (2 Kings 5:12), which rises in the Antilebanon and flows through Damascus] two Dough-offerings. . . . From the River and from Amanah, inwards, two Dough-offerings [are given].

Legislation thus affected Syria. R. Akiba's rule, "the like of whatsoever is permitted to be done in the land of Israel may be done also in Syria," implies much discussion of this point. Akiba died in 132 C.E.

But it is not necessary to emphasize economic factors exclusively in this connection, important though they are. The roots of the emphasis on The Land are deep in the Tanak, as we have seen: it was the land of milk and honey (Exod. 3:8, etc.), Israel's lasting resting place (Deut. 12:9),

and God's own Land (Josh. 22:19, etc.). After the horrors
of wars in the first and second centuries, and their subsequent dispersion, it was natural for rabbis to idealize the
old life in The Land before the wars. The Tannaitic and
other rabbinic sources, building on the Scriptures, point to
the significance of The Land in the most unambiguous
way, even if stimulated by economic and political realities.
There is a kind of "umbilical cord" between Israel and The
Land. It is no accident that one-third of the Mishnah, the
Pharisaic legal code, is connected with The Land. Nine-
tenths of the first order of the Mishnah, *Zeraim* (Seeds), of
the fifth order, *Kodashim* (Hallowed Things), and of the
sixth order, *Toharoth* (Cleannesses), deal with laws concerning The Land, and there is much of the same in the
other parts of the Mishnah. This is no accident, because for
the rabbis the connection between Israel and The Land was
not fortuitous, but part of the divine purpose or guidance,
as was the Law itself. Consider the following passage, ascribed to a rabbi flourishing betwen C.E. 140 and 165, from
Lev. Rabbah 13:2:

R. Simeon b. Yohai opened a discourse with: "He rose and measured the earth" [Hab. 3:6]. The Holy One, blessed be He, considered all generations and he found no generation fitted to receive
the Torah other than the generation of the wilderness; the Holy
One, blessed be He, considered all mountains and found no
mountain on which the Torah should be given other than Sinai;
the Holy One, blessed be He, considered all cities, and found no
city wherein the Temple might be built, other than Jerusalem; the
Holy One, blessed be He, considered all lands, and found no land
suitable to be given to Israel, other than the Land of Israel. This
is indicated by what is written: "He rose and measured the earth—
and He released nations" [ibid.].

The choice of Israel and the Temple and of The Land was
deliberate, the result of Yahweh's planning; R. Simeon b.

Yohai's thought goes back to the beginning of things and finds Yahweh's purpose at work then. The connection between Yahweh, Israel, The Land, Sinai, the Temple is primordial: it is grounded in a necessity of the divine purpose and is, therefore, unseverable. And it is no wonder that the rabbis heaped upon The Land terms of honour and endearment. For them, The Land of Israel is called simply *Hâ-'âretz*, The Land; all countries outside it are *hûtz lâ-'aretz*, outside The Land. In *BT* Berakoth 5a we read: "It has been taught: R. Simeon b. Yohai [C.E. 140–65] says: The Holy One, blessed be He, gave Israel three precious gifts, and all of them were given only through sufferings. These are: The Torah, the Land of Israel, and the World to Come."

We have seen that behind the glorification of The Land stood passages in the Scriptures. But, in addition to this, two factors could not but unceasingly stamp The Land upon the consciousness of Israel. The first is that the Law itself, by which Jews lived, was so tied to The Land that it could not but recall The Land. As we have already stated, one-third of the Mishnah deals with The Land and all the agricultural laws in it—like those of Scripture itself—do so. Consider the following passages: Lev. 19:23 (*H*); 23:10 (*H*); 23:22 (*H*); 25:2 (*H*); Deut. 26:1. These passages make it clear that the agricultural laws are to apply "in The Land." Further, only in Palestine could there be cities of refuge, which were so important in the civil law (Num. 35:9 f.; Deut. 4:41 f.; 19:1 f.). True, there are laws not contingent upon The Land; and the distinction between these and their opposite was clearly recognized. But the reward for the observance of the laws was "life in The Land," as is implied in Mishnah Kiddushin 1:9–10.

9. Any religious duty that does not depend on the Land (of Israel) may be observed whether in the Land or outside of it; and

any religious duty that depends on the Land may be observed in the Land [alone]; excepting the laws of *Orlah*-fruit and of Diverse Kinds. E. Eliezer says: Also the law of new produce.

10. If a man performs but a single commandment, it shall be well with him and he shall have length of days and shall inherit the Land; but if he neglects a single commandment, it shall be ill with him and he shall not have length of days and shall not inherit the Land. He that has a knowledge of Scripture and Mishnah and right conduct will not soon fall into sin, for it is written, "And a threefold cord is not quickly broken." But he that has no knowledge of Scripture and Mishnah and right conduct has no part in the habitable world.

The Law itself, therefore, to use current terminology, might be regarded as an effective symbol of The Land: it served as a perpetual call to The Land.

But, secondly, precisely because it was The Land to which the Law most applied, The Land gained in sanctity. Consider the following passages from Mishnah Kelim 1:6–9.

6. There are ten degrees of holiness. The Land of Israel is holier than any other land. Wherein lies its holiness? In that from it they may bring [the offerings of] the omer [sheaf], the firstfruits, and the two loaves, which they may not bring from any other land.

7. The walled cities [of The Land of Israel] are still more holy, in that they must send forth lepers from their midst; moreover they may carry around a corpse therein wheresoever they will, but once it is gone forth [from the city] they may not bring it back.

8. Within the wall [of Jerusalem] is still more holy, for there [only] they may eat the lesser holy things and the second tithe. The Temple Mount is still more holy, for no man or woman that has a flux, no menstruant, and no woman after childbirth may enter therein. The Rampart is still more holy, for no gentiles and none that have contracted uncleanness from a corpse may enter therein. The Court of the Women is still more holy, for none that

had immersed himself the selfsame day (because of uncleanness) may enter therein, yet none would thereby become liable to a sin-offering. The Court of the Israelites is still more holy, for none whose atonement is yet incomplete may enter therein, and they would thereby become liable to a sin-offering. The Court of the Priests is still more holy, for Israelites may not enter therein, save only when they must perform the laying on of the hands, slaughtering, and waving.

9. Between the Porch and the Altar is still more holy, for none that has a blemish or whose hair is unloosed may enter there. The Sanctuary is still more holy, for none may enter therein with hands and feet unwashed. The Holy of Holies is still more holy, for none may enter therein save only the High Priest on the Day of Atonement at the time of the [Temple] service. R. Jose said: In five things is the space between the Porch and the Altar equal to the Sanctuary: for they may not enter there that have a blemish, or that have drunk wine, or that have hands and feet unwashed, and men must keep far from between the Porch and the Altar at the time of burning the incense.

In each case—in the reference to The Land, the walled cities of The Land, the wall of Jerusalem, the Temple Mount, the Rampart, the Court of Women, the Court of the Israelites etc.—it is the connection with an enactment of the Law that determines the degree of its holiness. And, for our purposes especially, it is noteworthy that it is the applicability of the Law to The Land in 1:6 that assures its special holiness. The implication is that Jewish sanctity is only fully possible in The Land: outside The Land, only strictly personal laws can be fulfilled, that is, the moral law, sexual law, sabbath law, circumcision and dietary laws, etc. Of necessity, outside The Land, the territorial laws have to be neglected. Exile is, therefore, an emaciated life, even though, through suffering, it atones. A passage in *BT* Sotah 14a expresses this point of view in dealing with Moses' failure to enter The Land.

In the light of the above, it is not surprising that both the gift of prophecy—the gift of the Holy Spirit, and the gift of resurrection of the dead—were by some connected with The Land. Mekilta Pisha 1 both affirms Israel as the only land fit for prophecy and the dwelling of the Shekinah, and reveals the efforts made to deal with the difficulties such a position confronted; for example, the fact that Yahweh had appeared outside The Land.[11]

Again, in the view of some rabbis, the resurrection was to take place first in The Land, and the benefits of The Land in death are many (see Gen. Rabbah 96:5). Some urged that those who died outside The Land would not rise: but even an alien (Canaanitish) slave girl who dwelt in The Land might expect to share in the resurrection (see *BT* Ketuboth 111a). At the end of the second century, Rabbi Meir, at his death, required that his remains should be cast into the sea off the Palestinian coast, lest he be buried in foreign soil. There is no space or necessity here to enlarge further. The desire to die in The Land, to possess its soil, to make pilgrimages to it, all these manifestations of attachment to The Land history attests. The archaeological and literary

---

11. To the materials in *GL*, add a passage pointed out to me by Mr. Dale C. Allison from Pseudo-Philo (see M. R. James, ed., *Liber Antiquitatum Biblicarum,* p. 95):

4. And before all of them will I choose my servant Abram, and I will bring him out from their land, and lead him into the land which mine eye hath looked upon from the beginning when all the dwellers upon earth sinned before my face, and I brought on them the water of the flood: and then I destroyed not that land but preserved it. Therefore the fountains of my wrath did not break forth therein, neither did the water of my destruction come down upon it. For there will I make my servant Abram to dwell, and I will make my covenant with him, and bless his seed, and will be called his God for ever.

See also N. Avigad and Y. Yadin, eds., *The Genesis Apocryphon*; and Genesis Rabbah 33:6–7 on Gen. 8:10.

evidence that Jews from the Diaspora frequently arranged to be buried in Eretz Israel is clear for both the Tannaitic and Amoraic periods.[12]

Throughout the centuries, beginning with the fall of Jerusalem in C.E. 70, the conscious cultivation of the memory of The Land, concentrated in Jerusalem and the Temple, has continued in Judaism. The rabbis at Jamnia, in demanding that the Eighteen Benedictions (the Tefillah or Shemoneh Esreh) should be said three times a day—morning, afternoon, and evening (Mishnah Berakoth 4:1 ff.), had in mind, among other things, the perpetual remembrance of Jerusalem and The Land. The Shemoneh Esreh for the morning and afternoon service corresponded to the morning and afternoon daily whole-offerings in the Temple. There was no time fixed for the evening Shemoneh Esreh, but on sabbaths and festivals, the Shemoneh Esreh was to be said four times (there being demanded an additional Tefillah corresponding to the "additional offering" presented on those days in the ancient Temple). Three times daily, then, the Jew was required to pray; among other things, he was required to repeat the 14th Benediction (dated by Dugmore to 168–65 B.C.E.), the 16th (possibly pre-Maccabean), and the 18th (C.E. 40–70). These read as follows (they are modified in later Jewish prayer books):

Benediction 14

Be merciful, O Lord our God, in Thy great mercy, towards Israel Thy people, and towards Jerusalem Thy city, and towards Zion the abiding place of Thy glory, and towards Thy temple and Thy habitation, and towards the kingdom of the house of David, Thy

12. See Eric M. Meyers, *Jewish Ossuaries*, pp. 72–79. He also cites passages indicating resentment against second burials in Eretz Israel.

righteous anointed one. Blessed art Thou, O Lord God of David, the builder of Jerusalem.

Benediction 16

Accept [us], O Lord our God, and dwell in Zion; and may Thy servants serve Thee in Jerusalem. Blessed art Thou, O Lord, whom in reverent fear we serve [or, worship].

Benediction 18

Bestow Thy peace upon Israel Thy people and upon Thy city and upon Thine inheritance, and bless us, all of us together. Blessed art Thou, O Lord, who makest peace.

That there was a deliberate concern with Jerusalem appears from the text in Mishnah Berakoth 4:1 ff., where the rules concerning the Shemoneh Esreh, indicated above, are set forth, and where Mishnah Berakoth 4:5 states that, according to R. Joshua (C.E. 80–120),

If [a man] was riding on an ass [when the time for the prayer is upon him] he should dismount [that is, to say the Tefillah]. If he cannot dismount he should turn his face [toward Jerusalem]; and if he cannot turn his face, he should direct his heart toward the Holy of Holies.

The centrality of The Land is clear. The same is also emphasized in Num. Rabbah 23:7 on Num. 34:2. The deliberate recalling of the Temple and, thereby of Jerusalem and The Land, in the liturgy also appears from the Mishnah Rosh-ha-Shanah (the Feast of the New Year) 4:1–3. There were other ways by which the same purpose was achieved (see *BT* Baba Bathra 60b).

Other elements in the Jewish liturgy also commemorate the destruction. For three weeks of sorrow, ending on the ninth day of Ab, the fifth month of the Jewish calendar (July 8–August 7 to August 6–September 5), which is entirely given over to fasting, Jews annually recall the devastation of their Land and of Jerusalem. So much has that event become the quintessence of the suffering of Jewry that the 9th of Ab is recognized as a day on which disasters again and again struck the Jewish people. The essential feature of the liturgy for the 9th of Ab (which is the only twenty-four-hour fast, apart from the Day of Atonement) was the reading of lamentations and dirges. Later, on the fast of the 9th of Ab, an addition which concentrates on Jerusalem still further was made to the service. The prayer, as used today, begins with the words:

> O Lord God, comfort the mourners of Zion;
> Comfort those who grieve for Jerusalem.

It ends with:

> Praised are You, O Lord, who comforts Zion
> Praised are You, who rebuilds Jerusalem.

The reference to the festival of Ab leads naturally to the significance of the Jewish calendar for our purposes. That sabbaths and festivals and the rites of the faith should be accurately observed according to the Torah was a serious matter with cosmic consequences, because of the relation between the cultus and the cosmos; hence the importance of the Jewish religious calendar. Ideally, the sabbaths and the festivals should everywhere be observed at the same time, because there could only be one proper, ordained time. But this created problems. The communities in Babylonia or Asia Minor, for example, could not know— in the absence of communication systems such as our present ones—whether the month of Ellul had been declared hollow or full in Palestine. The ripening of barley did not come at the same time in Egypt, Babylonia, and Palestine. The Jewish religious calendar did not take into account the differences of time between Palestine and other countries.

This difficulty was recognized as early as 124 B.C.E. (2 Macc. 1:9). The authorities in Jerusalem tried to synchronize the dates of festivals in Jerusalem and the Diaspora. Mesengers were sent to the Diaspora to this end (1 Macc.1:9). Fires were used as signals from one region to another to indicate the incidence of the new moon in Jerusalem. Moreover, with the exception of the Day of Atonement, the sages doubled every festival day in the Diaspora to ensure against a margin of possible error. By such means, Jews in the Dispersion could believe that the prayers offered by them went up to heaven at the same time as those in The Land. That the effort to observe the same calendar outside The Land as in The Land involved religious Jews in incongruous and sometimes bizarre situations is familiar.

The religious calendar of Jews everywhere, then, was governed by that observed in The Land. But so, too, was the physical structure of the Jewish institution which was next in importance to the Temple and which after 70 C.E. came to replace the Temple, the synagogue. To this day, those who pray in a synagogue turn towards Jerusalem. In the synagogues of Galilee, in order to pray towards Jerusalem, one had to turn around. In other parts of Palestine in the first century, synagogues had three entrances on the side facing Jerusalem (although synagogues in the Golan Heights had no uniform arrangement). Later, the recess for the Ark of the Torah was placed in the wall facing Jerusalem, and in the Byzantine period the apses of synagogues were built to face Jerusalem.[13]

So far, we have mostly adduced materials from the Haggadah and the liturgy of rabbinic Judaism. There was also a more specifically halakic approach to the question of The

13. On the synagogue, see F. Hüttenmeister and G. Reeg, *Die antiken Synagogen in Israel*.

Land. We can here only refer to two items. In the Jerusalem Talmud, in Kilayyim 7:5, there is a law which is quoted as giving to Israel a legal right to The Land. This is translated by Lieberman as: "Though soil cannot be stolen, a man can forfeit his right to this soil by giving up hope of ever regaining it." The argument is that the people of "Israel" "never for a moment gave up hope of regaining the soil of Palestine. Never did they renounce their right to Palestine and never have they ceased claiming it in their prayers and in their teachings. It is on this foundation," adds Lieberman, "that [Jews] now claim that Eretz Israel belongs to [them]."[14] Not unrelated to this law is that of *ḥazâkâh* (prescription) in which the legal right of Israel to The Land was sought. How early such attempts were, and how significant in the discussion of the relationship between Israel and Eretz Israel in the period of our concern, we cannot determine. The history of the halakic understanding of that relationship lies beyond the scope of this study.

Be that as it may, it is in the Haggadah and the liturgy that the full force of the sentiment for The Land is to be felt. It cannot properly be seen except through Jewish eyes, nor felt except through Jewish words, such as those so powerfully uttered by Abraham Heschel in *Israel: An Echo of Eternity*, a book which is more a lyrical outburst than a critical study, and by André Neher in a moving essay, "Israël, terre mystique de l' Absolu," in his *L' Existence Juive*.

THE LAND IN SECONDARY SOURCES

So far, we have referred to the evidence of the classical sources of Judaism. The same theological conviction that there is an unseverable connection among Israel, The Land, and its God continued to be cherished throughout the me-

14. S. Lieberman, "Response," p. 287.

dieval period and down to the modern. A rough division
has been drawn between two periods. The first stretches up
to the last revolt of Jews in the Roman empire in the hope
of reestablishing a Jewish state. This followed upon the
imposition of harsh anti-Jewish statutes under Justinian
(483–565 C.E.), and later the brief reign in Jerusalem of
Nehemiah, a messianic figure, from 614 to 617 C.E. It is
legitimate to recognize, up to that time, a living, if inter-
mittent, hope for, and sometimes violent activity directed
towards, the actual return of The Land politically to Israel.
After the Arab conquest of The Land in 638 and the building of the Mosque of Omar, which was to be a center of
Islamic faith, on the site of the Temple in 687–91, there
was, it has been suggested, a change. From then Jewish
devotion to The Land for a long period expressed itself not
so much in political activity for the reestablishment of the
state of Israel as in voluntary individual pilgrimages and
immigrations to The Land.

But the division suggested between the two periods indicated must not be viewed as watertight. On the one hand,
in the earlier period the Tannaitic and Amoraic sages were
wary of political attempts to reestablish the kingdom of
Israel in its own Land. On the other hand, in the Middle
Ages, there was much activity aimed at such a reestablishment: the history of this has been largely lost, so that
its full strength must remain conjectural. The extent to
which apocalyptic messianism persisted, to break out
finally in Sabbatianism in the seventeenth century, is only
now being recognized, under the influence particularly of
the great work of Gershom Scholem. It fed into the Zionist
movement of our time. What we can be certain of is that
Eretz Israel, as an object of devotion and intense and religious concern, continued to exercise the imagination of
Jews after the fall of Jerusalem in 70 C.E. and after the Arab

conquest: it remained part of the communal consciousness of Jews.

In this connection, two facts need to be borne in mind. First, the devotion to The Land to which we refer is not simply to be equated with the imaginative notions of other peoples about an ideal land—such as the Elysium of Homer, the Afallon of Celtic mythology, or the Innisfree of Yeats. Rather, it was concentrated on an actual land with a well-known history, a land known to be barren and rugged and to offer no easy life, although it was transfused with an unearthly glory because chosen to be Yahweh's own, and Israel's as an inheritance from him. Secondly, the influence of the familiar or customary division of history at the advent of Christ into two periods, B.C. and A.D., has often tended to create the unconscious assumption among Gentiles that after the first century, Jews *as a people* ceased to have a common history. No less a scholar than Martin Noth saw Israel's history as having come to a ghastly end with the Bar Kokba revolt.

But the Jews continued not simply as a conglomerate of individuals but as a people. The Talmud, the primary document of Judaism in the Middle Ages and afterwards, up to the present time, concerns itself with the way in which the people of Israel should "walk." The Talmud has a communal national reference in its application of the Torah to the actualities of the Jews' existence. Its contents, formation, and preservation presuppose the continuance of the self-conscious unity of the people of Israel. It is this that explains the character of the Talmud: it adds Gemara to Mishnah, and Rashi (1040–1105 C.E.) to both, to make the tradition of the past relevant to the present. It is realistically involved with the life of the Jewish people over a thousand years of history.

In the devotional life of the Jewish community, the relationship to The Land also remained central. To trace the various expressions of devotion to The Land among Jews across the centuries is beyond our competence. The most noteworthy is, perhaps, that of pilgrimage. The Law demanded that every male Israelite should make a pilgrimage to Jerusalem three times a year, at Passover, the Feast of Weeks, and Tabernacles (Exod. 23:17; Deut. 16:16). During the Second Temple period, even Jews of the Diaspora sought to observe this demand. (See, for example, Mishnah Aboth 5:4; Mishnah Taanit [Days of Fasting] 1:3; Jos., *Wars* 6.9.) After the destruction of the Temple in 70 C.E., pilgrimages especially to the Wailing Wall became occasions for mourning: there were pilgrimages throughout the Middle Ages to other holy places. Individual Jews witness to this, a most famous expression coming in the works of the "God-intoxicated" or "God-kissed" Jehudah Halevi (ca. 1075–1141 C.E.), a Spanish physician and philosopher born in Toledo. At the age of fifty, he left his beloved Spain on a perilous pilgrimage to Zion. Possibly he died before reaching Jerusalem, but not before expressing his love for The Land and Zion in unforgettable terms such as:

My heart is in the east, and I in the uttermost west—
How can I find savour in food? How shall it be sweet to me?
How shall I render my vows and my bonds while yet
Zion lieth beneath the fetter of Edom, and I in Arab chains?
A light thing would it seem to me to leave all the good things of
    Spain—
Seeing how precious in mine eyes it is to behold the dust of the
    desolate sanctuary.[15]

15. *Selected Poems of Jehudah Halevi*, ed. H. Brody, p. 2. Professor Diez Macho of Madrid has pointed out that Halevi was not an isolated figure, but part of a tendency—if not a movement—in his day. Because of his profound yearning for Zion, Halevi has been called the father of Zionism or the first of the Zionists. For

It was not only single, individual pilgrims who sought The Land, but groups of communities, as in the case of Rabbi Meir of Rothenburg, who in 1286 C. E. sought to lead a great number of Jews from the area of the Rhine to Israel. Later, in 1523, a messianic movement which aimed at a return to The Land was led by David Reuveni and attracted the interest of communities in Egypt, Spain, and Germany. The living Jewish concern to establish an earthly kingdom in Jerusalem in part probably prompted the seventeenth article of the Confession of Augsburg of 1530. The justification for such a reaction was made luminously clear in the astounding response to the Sabbatian movement from the Yemen to Western Europe.[16]

These data to which historians point us cannot be ignored. The relative weight which should be given to the purely *religious* interest in The Land which led individuals and groups to journey to Israel out of a desire to experience its mystical or spiritual power, as against a political concern to escape and to right the wrongs of exile, we are not competent to assess. Certainly, many pious Jews had no directly political concern: their sole aim was to recognize

---

him, the prophet, not the philosopher, is the highest type of human being, and prophecy can only be experienced in Eretz Israel.

16. The pertinent part of Article 17 of the Augsburg Confession of 1530 reads as follows:

[The churches, with common consent among us] condemn the Anabaptists who think that to condemned men and devils shall be an end of torments. They condemn others also, who now scatter Jewish opinions, that, before the resurrection of the dead, the godly shall occupy the kingdom of the world, the wicked being everywhere suppressed [the saints alone, the pious, shall have a worldly kingdom, and shall exterminate all the godless]. [P. Schaff, ed., *Creeds of Christendom*, III, *Evangelical Creeds*, p. 18.]

that in The Land a relationship to the eternal was possible as nowhere else. A striking illustration of spiritual concentration on The Land is provided by Rabbi Nahman of Bratzlov, who journeyed to Israel in 1772–80. He asserted that what he had known *before* that journey was insignificant. *Before* there had been confusion; after "he held the Law whole." But all he had desired was simply direct contact with The Land. This he achieved by merely stepping ashore at Haifa. He desired to return immediately. (Under pressure, he stayed and visited Tiberias, but never even went up to Jerusalem.) Again, the celebrated Maharal of Prague (Rabbi Yehuda Liwa of Loew—Ben Bezalel, 1515–1609) understood the nature and role of nations to be ordained by God, as part of the natural order. Nations were intended to cohere rather than to be scattered. Nevertheless, he did not urge political reestablishment of a state of Israel in The Land: that he left to God. Exile, no less than restoration, was in His will: the latter *would* come in His good time, but only then. The promise of The Land would endure eternally: return was ultimately assured (Lev. 26:44–45).

At no time since the first century has The Land of Israel been wholly without a Jewish presence, however diminished. The figures throughout the centuries have been very variously estimated, but James Parkes rightly insists that Jews in Palestine across the centuries have been forgotten by historians. It is certain that in the nineteenth century, first under the influence of Rabbi Elijah, Ben Solomon Salman of Vilna, known as the Vilna Gaon (1720–97), a number of parties of Jews, soon to be joined by many others, went to Safed in 1808 and 1809. These sought not simply contact with The Land, of which they claimed that "Even in its ruins none can compare with it," but permanent settlement. Regarding themselves as representa-

tives of all Jews, they assumed the right to appeal to other
Jews for aid and reinforcement. Some—as in the case of
Rabbi Akiba Schlessinger of Pressburg (1837–1922)—were
driven to go to The Land, where alone the good life was
fully possible, by the realization of the increasing impos-
sibility of living according to the Torah in Western societies
which were becoming more and more secular. For such,
The Land became an escape and a refuge from modernism
and secularism, a bulwark for the preservation of the religious tradition. After these early settlements, there were
other efforts by religious Jews to reenter The Land, whose
history cannot be traced here. Suffice it to note that the
Zionist movement, despite its strongly "nationalistic," socialistic, and political character, is not to be divorced from
this devotion to The Land.[17] We shall deal with this later.

17. This remains true. But the concentration on The Land
among religious Jews who revered and even went to Eretz Israel
has also to be distinguished from the purely historical, geographical, and archaeological interest of many Zionists (see, especially,
D. Vital, *The Origins of Zionism,* pp. 6 ff.). Here we are dealing
with Judaism and The Land, not with Jews and The Land. But the
impression must not be given that these two themes can—or
should—be effectively separated. R. J. Werblowsky illustrates the
problem. He points out that in the nineteenth century assimi-
lationist Jews were fascinated and blinded by the Enlightenment.
In their enthusiasm for assimilation,they shed both their religious
and national identities. But they soon discovered the falsity of
their hopes of being fully integrated and "normalized" in Western
society. In disillusioned reaction to the society that had erstwhile
been so seductively attractive to them, they turned again to the
tradition they had shed. But for "enlightened" and "assimila-
tionist" Jews to rediscover and to return all at once to both their
religious and national identities was hardly possible: the rediscovery of *one* element of their tradition was traumatic; to have
discovered *both* at the same time would have been too overwhelming. So it was that the "enlightened" Jews who saw the

futility of assimilation turned, under the influence of the intellectual climate of the nineteenth century, first to "nationalism," socialism, and romanticism: they rediscovered themselves as belonging to the people of Israel, to a "national" tradition, not necessarily to the religion of Israel, which they still found it easy to regard as a fossilized survival. Even Werblowsky seems able to think of liturgical practice somewhat in these terms, writing of the belief in the relationship between Israel and The Land: "Très souvent, il était à la fois vivant et 'gélé,' comme dans une chambre froide, par les prières chaque jour répétées, les formules liturgiques et le rappel des promesses prophetiques" ("Israël et Eretz Israël, p. 377).

All this helps to explain the insensitivity of some of the leaders both before and in the Zionist movement to the strictly religious dimension of the relation to The Land. Of the Zionist leaders, Werblowsky writes: "Beaucoup d'entre eux ne pouvaient faire qu'une seule découverte a la fois" (ibid,. p. 388). For secular Jews in the nineteenth century, religious devotion to The Land symbolized all that was particularistic, "scandalous," and nonassimilable in Judaism, even when they themselves ultimately became Zionists.

2
An Undeniable Historical Diversity

> Whoever goes up from Babylon to the Land of
> Israel transgresses a positive commandment, for it
> is said in Scriptures, *They shall be carried to*
> *Babylon, and there they shall be, until the day that I*
> *remember them, saith the Lord.* Ketuboth 110b–111a
> (Babylonian Talmud)

We have sought in the preceding pages to do justice to the theological role of territory in Judaism. Jewish theology, as revealed in its major witnesses, points to The Land as of the essence of Judaism. In strictly theological terms, the Jewish faith might be defined as "a fortunate blend of a people, a land and their God." But in any blend, an ingredient may be submerged, and in this formula, it has been claimed, the essential and distinctive significance of The Land may be lost sight of. As the personal identity of each member is carefully preserved in discussions of the Trinity, and not simply "blended," so, too, in our understanding of Judaism, the distinct or separable significance of The Land must be fully recognized. Judaism held to an election of a people and of its election to a particular land: Werblowsky rightly speaks of "une vocation, spirituelle à la géographie."[1] But

1. R. J. Werblowsky, "Israël et Eretz Israël." In "Réflexions sur la pensée nationale juive moderne," Nathan Rotenstreich emphasizes the newness of Zionism or modern Jewish nationalism. It is, for him, discontinuous with traditional Jewish religious thought: "It attempts to create a new Jewish unity with living

like Christian, Jewish theology has had to find ways of coming to terms with history.

JEWISH PLURALISM

In the first place, the term "Judaism" itself cannot be understood as representing a monolithic faith in which there has been a simplistic uniformity of doctrine—whether demanded, imposed, or recognized—about The Land, as about other elements of belief. Certainly this was so at all periods and in all sections of the Jewish community before 70 C.E. To substantiate this point, we shall appeal to: (a) the rôle of the nomadic ideal of the desert in the Tanak; (b) the nature of the revolts in the Maccabean period and in the first century C.E.; (c) the place of Abraham in the Tanak; (d) Israel as a covenanted community; (e) the universal emphasis of many postexilic writers; (f) individualism; and (g) The Land as a symbol of the transcendental.

(a) As we have already seen, the rightness of Israel's conquest of Canaan did not go unquestioned. But the cruelty of the conquest apart, the antipathy which is endemic and

_____

institutions rooted in the present rather than surviving to the present" (p. 5). He therefore connects Zionism with the collapse of the foundations of traditional Jewish life, which succumbed to the attack on the traditional authorities, grounded in a supra-historical authority, of the Enlightenment (pp. 3–4). One can hardly agree that Zionism is so utterly newborn. As will be clear from the presentation, Zionism is in this book viewed as "twice-born," in the sense that it was preceded by a long tradition of concentration on The Land. (On its religious dimension, see Rolf Rendtorff, "Die religiosen und geistigen Wurzeln des Zionismus.") This does not mean that the precise forerunners of Zionism can be easily categorized (see Jacob Katz, "The Forerunners of Zionism," pp. 10–21). For a balanced and thorough treatment, see Ben Halpern, *The Idea of the Jewish State*, pp. 3–19, 55–94, and especially 95–130.

universal between those who follow a nomadic way of life and those who "indulge" in the sedentary, agricultural way is evident in the Tanak. In Gen. 4:1–17, for example, Cain, the tiller of the soil, who first built a city, is at a disadvantage against Abel, who was simply a keeper of sheep, not a full nomad. The offering of the firstlings of the flock is held to be more acceptable than that of the fruits of the soil. While it is doubtful whether the patriarchs were strictly nomadic, they did represent the classic simplicity of the ideal human life.

The role of the wilderness in the history of Israel has to be carefully noted. There are verses (Hos. 9:10; Ezek. 16:5; Jer. 31:2; and, less clearly, Deut. 32:10) where the wilderness period, as such, seems to be regarded as the decisive phase of that history—that is, the period of Israel's election. But usually the "wilderness" is inextricably bound up with the Exodus, the events at Sinai, and the wanderings. In the wilderness, Israel had experienced danger in obeying God's word and help in that danger (Exod. 13:17–14:31; 19:4, etc.): there, according to *J* and *E*, the revelation of God's name had been received (Exod. 3:13 [*E*]; Exod. 3:1 [*E*]; Exod. 33, 34 [*J*]), on the knowledge of which depended the possibility and validity of Israelite worship. There also the covenant had been established and the Law given, the foundations, along with the revelation of the name, of Israelite religion and Judaism. Through the covenant in the wilderness, with which the Law was inextricably bound up, Israel became the people of Yahweh (see Deut. 27:9 f.).[2] The desert is, therefore, the place of revelation and of the constitution of "Israel" as a people: there she was "elected" (Exod. 4:22 f.).

2. See also W. D. Davies, "Reflections on the Spirit in the Mekilta."

It is not surprising, therefore, that prophets looked back to the period in the wilderness for inspiration, as did Elijah (1 Kings 19:4–8). The time in the wilderness was regarded with nostalgia. Redemption was to be preceded by a return to the wilderness, where the old status of love and trust, broken by the "harlotry" of life in The Land, would be restored. (Hos. 2:14–15; cf. Heb. 2:16–17). The return to the wilderness is a return to the grace of God. Such a return is not envisaged by Jeremiah, but he also regards the time of the wilderness as one of mutual love between Israel and Yahweh (Jer. 2:1 f.). The time of the wilderness was one in which Israel had found grace (Jer. 31:2; cf. Exod. 33:12 f., 16 f.). There is also an appeal to that time as the norm against which to judge the corruption of the sedentary life, a corruption that was bound up with cultus that had evolved in The Land (Amos 5:25 and Jer. 7:21–23). In Isa. 63:10–14, the time in the wilderness had been marked by the presence of the Spirit. But, more important still, the response to the challenge of Canaanite religion to Yahwehism in some circles took the form of a complete rejection of settled agricultural life as the will of Yahweh for his people. This was the position of the Rechabites, who appear as a vital group as late as the sixth century B.C.E. They would not grow cereals, cultivate the vine, or live in houses. True, they did live in Judah, but the Hebrew text at Jer. 35:7 makes it clear that they regarded themselves merely as sojourners who had no original rights in The Land. That they lived in tents, not in houses, marks them as deliberately nomadic: the tent is the nomadic abode, a symbol of nomadic opposition to sedentary culture, which was deemed to be unmanly and degrading (compare the attitude revealed in the story of the blessing of Jacob and Esau in Gen. 27:11: Esau is a hairy man and Jacob a smooth man). The Rechabites' total abstinence from wine was not so much a moral protest against drunken Canaanite orgies connected with fertility rites (although such a protest is not to be excluded) as an affirmation of the nomadic life, in which wine was not drunk. There are counterparts to the Rechabites among the Nabataeans.

By the time of Jeremiah, although, in the prophet's view, admirably active, the Rechabites had dwindled to a few: the prophet could invite them all to meet him in a chamber in the Temple (Jer. 35:2). There is meagre evidence that they did survive the Exile, but it is more likely that they increasingly succumbed to the ways of the majority in Israel. There are no traces of them in the New Testament itself.

It is not impossible, however, that the Rechabites stood in some connection with the Nazirites, about whom we do read in the New Testament. The origins and purposes of the Nazirites are obscure. But they have been understood as representatives of the opposition to the Canaanization of the cult of Yahweh. The Nazirite avoidance of wine was possibly bound up with a suspicion of the land of the vine, the symbol of the agricultural as against nomadic life (Amos 2:11–12; Num. 6).

However, the requirement of the presentation of a cereal offering in Num. 6:17 on the completion of the Nazirites' time of separation should warn us against pressing this point. And, in any case, the significance of the Rechabites and Nazirites should not be overemphasized. They were few in number, and at no time did they represent the mind of Israel. Jeremiah's commendation of the Rechabites (35:18–19) referred not to their way of life as such, but to their fidelity to that to which they were committed: he cherished a like fidelity for Israelites generally to the commandments to which *they* were committed.

The attempt to claim, on the basis of the material we have presented above, and of other factors which we cannot consider here, that Israel had a nomadic ideal of life must be rejected. To begin with, the passage from Amos which has been taken to suggest this has been otherwise explained. Thus, Amos 5:25 does not necessarily mean that Amos questioned the Mosaic origin of the sacrificial system, and probably does not involve any idealization of the period in the wilderness.

This alternative interpretation of Amos 5:25 affords a convenient point of transition to other passages which present the time of the wilderness and the wilderness itself in a cold light, without any idealization. We find a clear-eyed recognition of the wilderness period as marked by rebellion. It was a time of "murmuring." The long and dangerous journey through the wilderness had not been the free choice of Israel, but the outcome of a command by Yahweh (Exod. 3,4): it had not been voluntary, simply a matter of obedience. In the course of it, there were trials to Israel's faith—Pharaoh and his army (Exod. 14: 10f.), lack of water (Exod. 15:24; 17:2), of bread (Exod. 16:2 f.), and the giants barring entrance to The Land (Num. 14:2 f.). These all led to disobedience to Moses, the leader; to Aaron, his mouthpiece; and to Yahweh himself (Exod. 15:24; 16:2; 17:2; Num. 14:2): Israel tired of the wilderness life (Num. 21:5). The "murmuring" reached its culmination in the worship of the golden calf (Exod. 32), the significance of which is manifold. The bull or calf is a prominent image of Canaanite fertility worship: the seduction of the latter, so we are to understand, had already exerted itself in the wilderness. By the worship of the golden calf, Israel revealed her preference for many gods (Exod. 32:4) and practically revoked her covenant with Yahweh. The election of Israel was all but annulled (Exod. 32:10) and was preserved only by the renewal of the covenant in Exod. 34. The point is that the wilderness was as much a scene of sin as of election.

In Deuteronomy, the time of the wanderings is used for purposes of exhortation, as in Deut. 8:2–5. Here there is no idealization of the time in the wilderness. Rather, it was then that Yahweh had tested, disciplined, and humbled Israel, leading her to the knowledge that she lived solely by his word and to the humility springing from this. There is no glorification of the simple nomadic life and the wilderness in themselves. Rather, a *time* is remembered which, as Deut. 8:7 ff. makes clear, prepared Israel for life in The Land.

Emphasis on the time in the wilderness as one of terrible punishment and discipline and warning appears in Psalms. That time is seldom referred to—as surely might be expected in view of Yahweh's providential succour, guidance, and election—in psalms of praise and thanksgiving. Where it is referred to in the latter, the generation of the wilderness is the supreme example of sinfulness. Psalms 78, 95, and 106 are particularly instructive.

The connection between the period of the wilderness and the Exile is also made in Ezek. 20:23. The prophet goes so far as to claim that at that time, in order that Israel might know that he was the Lord, Yahweh had given her "statutes that were not good and ordinances by which they could not have life" (20:25): He had deliberately defiled and horrified his people (20:26). And in Ezekiel there is also an echo of Deuteronomy's view of the time of the wilderness as a painful preparation for life in The Land. For him, in the future, before the redemption of Israel, the wilderness is to be the place of judgment, as it had been in the past (see Ezek. 20:33 ff.). We have previously noted in Hosea the notion of a return to the wilderness as a condition of renewal before entry into The Land. There a return to the time when Israel enjoyed filial status with Yahweh is signified: it provided a "door of hope." In Ezekiel, as we have seen, the wilderness is a place of judgment: the infidelity of the people in the period of the wanderings is reiterated unsparingly. But in Ezekiel the return to the wilderness is also a prelude to life in The Land and is, in this sense, a sign of hope. The way to The Land is through the wilderness. And this motif persisted.

In Deutero-Isaiah, the return of the dispersed to The Land is to be through a wilderness, the difficulties of which have been smoothed (Isa. 40:3 f.; 35:1 f., 6 ff.; 41:18 f.; 49:9 ff.): a way will appear through the wilderness (40:3; 43:19; 49:11). There is to be a new exodus, incomparably greater, even though the counterpart of the first. This notion later emerges in 1 Enoch 28:1, 29:1; and The Martyrdom of Isaiah 2:8–12. That it was understood not merely oratorically or metaphorically is clear from three sources.

First, the Dead Sea Scrolls. The community of the new covenant, by the location of its headquarters at Qumran in the desert, a location dictated by the text of Isa. 40:3; by its organization—into tribes, thousands, hundreds, fifties, and tens, which parallel the subdivision of Israel under Moses; and by the regulation of its life in camps (compare 1QM 7:3–7 with Num. 5:1–4) showed its concern to "return" in repentance to the wilderness in preparation for the redemption that would lead it to the purified Land. Secondly, in Josephus certain groups who *may* have had messianic pretensions, since they promised to repeat the "signs" or miracles of the first exodus, went into the desert to prepare for a coming redemption. So, too, a prophet from Egypt; Theudas; and a weaver, Jonathan, all had recourse to the desert to prepare for their assault on Jerusalem. And, in the last desperate hours of the war against Rome, the Jews asked for permission to leave the Temple for the desert with their wives and children, probably because they expected the final deliverance to be inaugurated there. In the light of the Dead Sea Scrolls, it seems clear that a retreat to the desert could easily be understood as a preparation for the messianic age. Finally, this is indicated in the New Testament itself by John the Baptist's preparatory ministry in the wilderness, and explicitly in Matt. 24:26.

It is of the utmost importance that the new covenanters at Qumran, John the Baptist, and the figures mentioned by Josephus, did not go into the wilderness because they valued it as such, but because they were thereby fulfilling what had become a kind of eschatological dogma that a time in the wilderness would precede the end. Their "return" to the wilderness was *not* governed by a rejection of "cultured" life in The Land in favour of a more simple nomadic existence in the desert, or by a geographic preference for the wilderness over The Land, but by an eschatological schema; not by considerations of space, but of time; not by the cult of the primitive, but by the observation of the times.

There is thus no justification for positing a nomadic ideal in the Tanak. Efforts to do so on the grounds of an idealization of the desert cannot be substantiated. The other grounds for doing so do not carry conviction, for reasons which cannot be set forth here. Our rejection of a nomadic ideal in the Tanak can be carried over into Judaism. True, the wilderness reappears in the eschatology of Judaism, in terms, among other things, of a new exodus which would witness a new Moses and the return of the manna, etc. But in that eschatology also, the wilderness is not the goal but a stage on the way to The Land, the glorification of which we have already illustrated from rabbinic sources.

(b) Most of the exiles in Babylon did not choose to return

to The Land when Cyrus (538 B.C.E.) made this possible.
Moreover, while the leaders of the returned community
were from Babylon, clearly The Land as such had little
appeal for them. It was not the returned exiles whom Haggai and Zechariah called upon to rebuild the Temple, but
native Israelites. And it should be emphasized that, after the
return from the Exile, Jews in Palestine itself were a
"dispersion." During the period after Nehemiah (432
B.C.E.) and before Alexander's conquest in 332 B.C.E., the
district of Judaea consisted simply of Jerusalem and a small
area, about thirty-five miles long and twenty-five to thirty
miles broad, surrounding it. Both within this tiny area and
outside it, Jews came to be surrounded by Hellenistic
influences. The temptation to assimilate was real and
ubiquitous. What was the attitude to The Land in this
period among Palestinian Jews thus exposed? Had it been
of vital significance, it is surprising that so little of a direct
appeal to The Land was made in the Maccabean revolt,
particularly since The Land itself had been so reduced. No
preeminence was given to Abraham and the promise. It
was the commandments of the Law, not the occupation of
The Land, that concerned the dying Mattathias, who had
initiated the revolt. It was so throughout his life. His rallying cry was simple: "Whosoever is zealous for the Law and
maintaineth the covenant, let him come forth after me."
And it was in this spirit that the volunteers, "a company of
Ḥasidim," who have been regarded as the fathers of the
Pharisees, offered themselves. The absence of an appeal to
The Land is striking because of the vividness of the awareness of the unity of the People of Israel in 1 Macc. It agrees
with this that, when appeal is made to history, it is not to
the promise to Abraham, but to the Exodus, the event that
gave birth to the people. Later on, territorial considerations
did enter into the Maccabean movement, but these were

motivated more by political ambition than by religious concern with the promise.

But the matter is even more puzzling, because there was a direct threat to confiscated Jewish lands under the Seleucids. The rural Jews, especially, would have been sensitive to the threat to their Land, and not only they, but all Jews in Judaea. This makes it all the more difficult to understand the absence of an appeal to The Land as such in our sources.

We note, in the second place, that a similar phenomenon—absence of a direct appeal to The Land—confronts us when we turn to the revolt against the Romans, culminating in the fall of Jerusalem in C.E. 70. There is a baffling lack of any direct appeal to the promise of The Land and to The Land itself. There are a few passages where appeal is made to the "laws of the country" or "of The Land," but it is religious loyalty and social, economic, and political pressures which spurred the rebels of the first century C.E., like those of the second century B.C.E., not an explicitly territorial concern. Is this to be interpreted as an indication that The Land as such was not a primary focus of concern? The argument from silence is precarious, however, for several reasons.

During both the Maccabean and Roman revolts, the people of Israel were dwelling in The Land, so that preoccupation with any conquest or occupation of it was not their immediate concern. Rather, it was the terms on which they were to live in The Land. What were these to be? Two desiderata had to be met to satisfy those in Israel who were "zealous."

First, it will be clear from what we have said before that Israel, as the covenant people, could only occupy The Land securely if the commandments were observed. The occupation of The Land presupposed loyalty to the Torah, which was a form of loyalty to The Land. Torah and Land are, if not inextricable, closely related. The threat to the Torah was in a tangible, though indirect, sense a threat to The Land. And when Israel actually dwelt in The Land, as in the Maccabean and Roman periods, the explicit concentration was naturally on the former.

Secondly, The Land was involved in any threat to the Temple. Life in The Land was regarded as integrally related to the cultus at Jerusalem. Changes in that cultus were particularly resented by the farmers in the rural areas, for whom the productivity of the soil was compromised by changes in Temple worship. It is no accident that the leadership in the Maccabean revolt was from the rural priesthood. They believed that on the observance of the Law, which included the observance of the festivals and Temple ritual, depended the well-being of The Land. It follows that, in periods when Israel actually dwelt in The Land, it was at the point of observance of the Torah and reverence for the Temple that concern for The Land expressed itself, albeit indirectly. This explains the centrality of Torah and Temple in the Maccabean and Zealot revolts, which in the minds of the rebels assumes the essentiality of The Land.

But what most threatened the loyalty due to Torah and Temple, through which the covenant people could enjoy life in the promised Land, was an alien occupying power. So long as the Seleucids or the Romans—or, indeed, any other power—ruled The Land, which belonged to Yahweh, so long would observance of the Torah and reverance for the Temple be precarious. It is in the light of this fact that the description of "the fourth philosophy," the Zealots, is to be understood in Josephus (see *Antiquities* 18. 1. 6).

History had taught the Jews in the Maccabean period, as in the Roman, that a foreign ruler could disrupt the conditions under which alone the covenant people could live in the promised Land. Even Josephus, despite his hatred of the Jewish nationalists, had to admit that they were very like the Pharisees. That is, although Josephus presented them in terms of "madness," they revered the Law and the Temple. Their peculiar emphasis (which doubtless the Pharisees shared *in principle,* although *in practice* they urged patience and long-suffering) that God alone was to be their ruler and Lord, sprang from the bitter history of Israel and clear-eyed recognition that they could only dwell securely in the promised Land when it was not occupied territory.

The story of the conquest and occupation of The Land under Joshua was vivid in the Maccabean mind and in that of the nationalists of the first century. The would-be return to the wilderness in both revolts points to this. Touched upon only briefly in 1 Macc. 2:29–30, the theme is noted in far more striking circumstances in Josephus's account of the fall of the Temple. After suicidal resistance, and finally the rejection of Titus's offer to enter into negotiations, the rebels wanted only "permission to pass through his line of circumvallation with their wives and children, undertaking to return to the desert and to leave the city to him." What is the explanation of this strange request? In all probability, the rebels were governed by the eschatological belief that before the final redemption, even after the Temple itself had been forsaken by the Lord, the Lord himself would not forsake his people, but continue his presence with them in the wilderness to lead them again into the promised Land. Like the Maccabees who withdrew to the wilderness, the Zealots also in their final request showed how the story of the conquest of The Land informed their thinking and activity.

Moreover, in the Maccabean period, at two points in Daniel, the interest in The Land may be claimed to break through indirectly. First, in Dan. 7:25–26, as part of the

description of the Fourth Beast, who is to be identified with
Antiochus Epiphanes, the saints of the Most High are to
endure the domination of the Fourth Beast "for a time, two
times, and half a time." The process of thought by which
this notion of three and a half years, or a very brief period,
arose has eluded commentators. But a suggestion by Bickerman is convincing. In three and a half years, the enemy
of the saints of the Most High would be "consumed and
destroyed to the end." On this Bickerman comments:
"Three years and a half is a half of the Sabbatical period.
According to the Law, the land of Israel had to have a
solemn rest every seven years and lie fallow. In Leviticus
(26:34–43) the desolation of the land under foreign domination appears as reparation for the lack of the sabbatic rest
under national rule. The Jews will have to suffer a half of
a sabbatic septennium in payment for their disobedience of
God's law."[3] If this suggestion be followed, the awareness
of The Land, its reactions and demands, was alive in the
Maccabean period. This is also implied in another passage
in Dan. 11:14–12:4. Here that Land is "the fairest of all
lands" (NEB, Dan. 11:16; compare 8:9). There is no doubt
that at the end The Land, "the fairest of all lands," remains
central, despite the cosmic horizons of Daniel. Antiochus
Epiphanes was to meet his doom, apparently, "between the
sea and the holy hill"—that is, between Jerusalem and the
sea (11:45), which Ezekiel (38:14–16; 39:2–4) had foretold
as the scene of the climax of all things. And it was in The
Land that the resurrection would take place (Dan. 12:1–3).

How, then, shall we assess the rôle of loyalty to The
Land in the Maccabean and Zealot revolts? Despite the
silence of the sources, it cannot be doubted that that loyalty
was a primary axiom for the rebels—our deepest axioms or

3. E. Bickerman, *Four Strange Books of the Bible*, p. 101.

assumptions are often most unexpressed. But it was un-expressed, too, because in both revolts it took a religious form, so that in the sources it is loyalty to the Torah and the Temple that is stressed.

The essence of the Maccabean revolt is clear. It was not a popular revolt of the whole people, the majority of whom seemed to have been ready to assimilate: The Land cannot have been primary for them. The revolt was the work of a small minority of enthusiasts for the Law and, implicitly, for The Land, who were as incensed by the apostates among their own people as they were with Antiochus. It seems that the majority of the tiny Jewish political unit around the city of Jerusalem, as well as the Jews in the rest of Palestine, who were surrounded by a sea of Hellenistic influences, cannot have been moved by loyalty to The Land. And as for the Ḥasidim who joined the Maccabean revolt, it is a familiar, but for our purposes a highly significant, fact that as soon as the religious aims of the revolt had been achieved, that is freedom to observe the Law, they withdrew from further participation. They had no territorial ambitions.

So also in the revolt against Rome in the first century. Josephus doubtless isolates the extremist leaders of the revolt against Rome too much in their ideology and activity. But it cannot be doubted that they constituted a minority, as did the Maccabean rebels. First-century Judaism is the creed of Hillel and Rabbi Johanan ben Zakkai—lovers of peace—no less than of the Zealots.

But the situation in Israel between the Exile and the first century was even more complicated than we have indi-cated. Let us return to the sectarians at Qumran, who dem-onstrate a concentration on The Land and the need for its purification. As we have seen, the Maccabees and the Zeal-ots hardly ever refer to The Land directly, whereas the sectarians regarded it as part of their very purpose to "atone for The Land." This difference probably has deep roots. Those who returned from Babylon, when Cyrus made this possible, were not a monolithic group. For many among them, the return to The Land and the rebuilding of the Temple signified Yahweh's favour. His judgments against Israel had now run their course. The restored community, devoted to the Law and the Temple, could count on his blessing. Life in The Land was the seal of divine favour. To the early days of the return belong those psalms which emphasize Jerusalem as the dwelling place of Yahweh, the centre of the theocracy of Israel.

Among those who thought in this way were the core of the Maccabean and later first-century rebels. They do not refer to The Land: they silently assume its importance and their right to it. They are not troubled by any sense that the people of Israel themselves had been responsible for defiling it. The Land needed no purification or atonement, only defence, when the Torah and its Temple were threatened from outside.

But there were others in postexilic Israel who differed. For these, although Israel had been given the opportunity to resettle in The Land, divine displeasure had not been exhausted. They still anticipated a dread future of further judgment upon Israel before the end should come. (For the way in which vengeance against sinful Israelites is often associated with the concept of The Land, see Jub. 15:28; 20:4; 21:22; 36:9; 50:5; and 2 Bar. 66:2, 5.) In postexilic Israel, those for whom Israel was a theocracy, which had "arrived," coexisted with those for whom it was still under the shadow of eschatology.

It is in the light of this discussion that the difference between the Maccabean and later nationalist movements and the sectarians at Qumran is to be understood. Let us recall the sectarians' understanding of themselves and of those around them. They were governed by their memory of the Exile, in which they found the model or parallel to their own experience. In that first exile in a foreign land, Yahweh had spared a remnant which had confessed its faults and returned to The Land under Ezra and Nehemiah. But the community which had since developed in The Land had not remained true to the demands of the covenant revealed by them: it had forsaken the revelation given to the remnant in and from Babylon. The Land had become polluted or defiled. Loyal to the commandments of the covenant of the remnant from the Exile, the sectarians, who continued that remnant, viewed the life of their countrymen, the sanctuary, and the priesthood at Jerusalem, with horror. Separation from Judah and Jerusalem became imperative. They must go into "exile." Exile was preferable to life in the defiled Land. Ephraim, in exile, became a revered prototype. The sectarians chose to leave Judah to go to "the land of Damascus"—into exile.

It is best to interpret "the land of Damascus" as referring to Qumran, not to Babylon. But Qumran was not simply a geographic centre. In fulfillment of Zech. 11:1 and Amos 7:15 "the land of Damascus" was a symbol of the land of deportation, "the land of the north." There Yahweh now had his sanctuary, not at Judah or Jerusalem: there he now gave his revelation and, there, in the end of days, a star, a leader, was to appear to lead the remnant back to Jerusalem purified through punishment. Through "the diaspora," "the exile" of the sectarians, salvation would come for The Land. The sect called itself "the exile," and saw Judah and Jerusalem, The Land, as profaned and in dire need of atonement. And this atonement was to come not from Jerusalem but from outside it. The true community of God was an exile through which alone The Land was to achieve atonement.

It is not impossible that those Jews who were still geographically exiles in the time of the sectarians influenced them. Not all had returned to The Land from Babylon. Were those who remained there influenced by the words of Jeremiah and Ezekiel as to the positive aspects of life in the Exile? Was it they who retained the traditions and thought of Baruch and Ezra? Some of them were of Davidic descent, some were priests of ancient lineage. They continued from afar to infuse new blood into Palestinian Judaism right down to the first century and much later. What was their attitude to the developments in Judah and Jerusalem after the return? We know that they regarded the Second Temple as tainted, and the question becomes inevitable whether there were continuing connections between the sectarians at Qumran, who regarded themselves as "exiles," and those others exiled in Babylon and elsewhere in the Diaspora. (In the "War of the Sons of Light and the Sons of Darkness," there is a clear indication of the sectarians' very wide range of concern [IQM 1:1–7; 2:1 ff.], the exiles in Babylon being included in the final war.) Was it to such connections that the sectarians owed the Iranian elements which their documents reveal? And was it to Babylon that those regulations in CDC which seem to envisage a foreign country apply? Were there Essenes in Babylon also, and did they share in a theology which perceived life outside The Land as making possible the emergence of a remnant to atone for The Land?

One thing may be regarded as certain. The uncritical, and assumed or implicit devotion to The Land which emerged in the Maccabean and Zealot mind was not unchallenged. True, for the sectarians also, especially as their mind is revealed in the Temple scroll, life in a purified Land and a purified city and Temple was the final goal, but they clearly saw that, in their present state, Land and city and Temple were defiled.

(c) The comparative paucity of references to Abraham and The Land in the Maccabaean and Roman revolts incites a prior question. Does the Tanak itself support the ascription of a controlling significance to the promise to Abraham? One serious difficulty is this: in the Tanak, outside the Pentateuch, the promise to Abraham as such is seldom referred to. Is it likely, therefore, to have played a significant, reassuring part in the faith of Israel?

The same paucity marks the Apocrypha and Pseudepigrapha.[4] We previously noted that the sources dealing with the Maccabees seldom refer to Abraham, and then not in connection with the promise of The Land. The same is true of the Apocrypha and Pseudepigrapha in general. Surprisingly, the same must be asserted even of the rabbinic sources. In the Mishnah there are hardly twelve references to Abraham, and among the early Midrashim, apart from Genesis Rabbah, where discussion of Abraham is inevitable, the patriarch is rarely discussed. It agrees with this that the covenant itself—because of the emphasis upon it in Christianity?—was seldom directly treated in early rabbinic sources. The covenant with Abraham was at the foundation—assumed and unexpressed—of the people of Israel. Like the foundation of a building, it was often hidden from view and not actively discussed. But it is erroneous to claim that Abraham and the covenant were a preoccupation of the Judaism revealed in the classical sources.

4. The Apocalypse of Abraham (80–100 C.E.) and the Testament of Abraham (early first century C.E.) do not concentrate on the promise of The Land.

(d) The people of Israel were essentially a covenanted community, but in the strictly religious sense. Our treatment of the relationship of the Law and The Land may have created the impression that Israel in the Tanak is to be understood as a community bound to a land and governed by a law, much as a modern national state might be so tied and governed. But one thing has emerged clearly from studies on law in the Hebrew Scriptures. The laws were not related primarily to the political organization of a state, but rather to a community of people in which the common allegiance to Yahweh was the constitutive element. The context or setting in life in which Israel had received the Law was the covenant, a sacral act, and the communication of the Law was connected with the celebration of the covenant which bound Israel to its God. To maintain the validity of this covenant—of which the proclamation of the Law was an essential part—Israel celebrated or commemorated it in regular feasts. In this religious act lay the foundation of Israel. "The Israelite nation, then, had its true existence apart from and prior to the erection of their political, social and economic order in Canaan."[5] The community is to be understood as a corollary of the covenant.

It is this that explains why it is difficult, if not impossible, to discover any Israelite idea of the state. The Israelites did not imitate the Canaanite principalities which they ousted. These principalities were made up of fortified cities surrounded by small territories: they were under a king, often of foreign birth, who led an army drawn from his own people and from mercenaries. But Gideon refused to be a king (Judg. 8:22 f.) (the kingdom of Abimelech, based on non-Israelite elements, was short-lived [Judg. 8:31; 9:1 f.]). In Canaan, Israel at first formed a federation

5. R. B. Y. Scott, *The Relevance of the Prophets*, p. 189.

of twelve tribes: these owed a common loyalty to Yahweh and shared a common law. But, to go by the Book of Judges, they had no organized government. The judges themselves were charismatic figures called by Yahweh for specific missions: they were not rulers of all Israel. In time, the Israelite federation became a national monarchical state under Saul. But such a state was not unopposed. The attitude toward the monarchy was divided. To some it was initiated by God: to others it was due to a reprehensible desire on Israel's part to be like other nations. Nevertheless, under David and Solomon, unity was achieved between Israel and Judah: the two areas were subsumed under one sovereign. But this state of affairs lasted only for two generations. On Solomon's death, Israel and Judah separated, and two kingdoms emerged. Sometimes they were allies: sometimes enemies. What is significant is that they acted independently, and that other nations treated them as two distinct powers. Political unity, a single statehood, eluded the people. At the same time, throughout the separation of the monarchy, the religious idea of the unity of the people, of the federation of the Twelve Tribes, remained. And the prophets, as we have seen, looked forward to their reunion. "Israel" and the political organization or organizations of its people are to be distinguished.

After 587 B.C.E., when Jerusalem fell, the idea of a state declined. The Jews became again mainly, if not purely, a religious community: in time priests came to rule them under God. Israel is the people of Yahweh alone. In Ezra and Nehemiah, the primary, if not the only, concern is that the people should obey the Law. If we follow the traditional view of the origin of the Ḥasidim, Pharisees, and Essenes, it was loyalty to the Law alone that governed them, and initially it was this that moved the Maccabees also. After the Exile, religious Jews became a people of the

Torah. The history of Pharisaism is necessarily concentrated much more on the Torah than on the political control of The Land.

The messianic ideas of Judaism, which have persisted from biblical to modern times, for example in Sabbatianism, have retained a political dimension, and one aspect, the national state, has remained central to them. But those ideas have often been spiritualized and transcendentalized and made symbolic. Without further elaboration, we shall assume here that the doctrine of the unseverability of The Land from Yahweh and his people is not to be too easily equated with the eternal connection of any state with the people and with Yahweh.

And yet, despite the data to which we have referred above and Scholem's apparent distinction between the political and the religious (see below), caution is necessary. There is the question which forcibly came to the surface among European peoples, not to be reinterred, in 1848: Can a people fully be itself without political self-expression or the right to self-determination (two concepts not usually distinguished), that is, without being allowed to be a nation? Is the distinction between a people living in The Land of Israel and the nation of Israel ultimately a false one? Does not its full life in The Land demand that the people of Israel control its own land? And there is the problem posed by the exact interpretation of the Jewish evidence. Usually the best guide to the inner life and meaning of a religious community is its liturgy. If so, in the most familiar and central prayer of Judaism, the Shemoneh Esreh, the distinction between life in The Land and "national" control of The Land is not recognized. The 14th Benediction, which is usually dated from the Maccabean period, reads: "Be merciful, O Lord our God, in Thy great mercy, towards Israel Thy people, and towards Jerusalem Thy city, and towards Zion the abiding place of Thy glory, and towards Thy temple and Thy habitation, and towards the kingdom of the house of David, Thy righteous anointed one. Blessed art Thou, O Lord God of David, the builder of Jerusalem." The reference to the kingdom of the house of David is unambiguous. For religious Jews, we must conclude, The Land is ultimately inseparable from the state of Israel, however much the actualities of history have demanded their distinction.

In this work, we are concerned not with the role of a Jewish state, but with that of The Land as such—that is, the promised Land. But we must issue the *caveat* that the distinction, although often necessarily recognized in Jewish life and thought, and therefore unavoidable in this discussion, is in the final analysis alien to the Jewish faith. To religious Jews, the separation of The Land and the state is the abortive product of Jewish history, not of Jewish religous consciousness and intent. And yet, despite the vicissitudes of Jewish history, the sacred documents on which religious Jews have based themselves—the Tanak, the Mishnah, the Midrashim, and the Talmud, the liturgies they have constantly celebrated, and the observances which they have kept across the centuries, all point to "The Land" itself, not, primarily at least, to any state, as the essential aspect of Judaism. We shall see that the leaders of Judaism were compelled by the experiences of their history to emphasize the religious, not the political, aspects of their faith; their covenantal status, not their aspirations to statehood.

(e) In many documents of the Tanak, the precise dating of most of which is difficult, but all of which are postexilic—Job, Proverbs, Ecclesiastes, the Song of Songs, Esther, Jonah, and even part of Daniel—The Land of Israel as such hardly plays any part. This is noteworthy. Especially in the postexilic period, when Jews inhabited The Land, the loss of political control in their country might have been expected to lead to a living concern with, if not concentration upon, the territorial doctrine if it had been very significant among them. To judge from the literature to which we have referred, however, this did not happen. Instead a concern with broad human problems, rather than specifically Israelite ones, is more in evidence.

The broad human concerns in the postexilic writings to which we have referred are not necessarily to be understood as precluding attachment to The Land. The postexilic period witnessed the work of the priestly "school" which formulated *P*. This certainly concentrated on Temple and Land, as had Ezekiel (although it is to be recognized that in Ezekiel and *P* there is also traceable a tendency to deny that the presence of Yahweh is to be associated with any single place). The Psalms bear witness to the love of The Land, and the author of 1 and 2 Chronicles enlarged the role of David (1 Chron. 17:14; 28:5; 29:23). But the fact remains that in the literature of the postexilic period there is an undeniable relocation of interest away from The Land to the broadly human. This is surprising at first, but fits in with another, frequently noted, development in the postexilic period.

(f) In that period there emerged, not a new, but a deepened awareness of the dimensions of specifically personal religious experience. The spiritual pilgrimage of the individual as such, not only as a member of the group, gained in significance. Jeremiah had prepared the way for this at the cost of the loneliness of his ministry: he seems to have felt at times that "the whole cause of Yahweh in the world hung on his individual life."[6] Ezekiel had come to recognize that, however much a part of the group, each Israelite stood

6. J. Skinner, *Prophecy and Religion*, p. 223.

alone. And in Deutero-Isaiah an interesting phenomenon already begins to confront us. The vocabulary of entry into The Land—that is, the vocabulary of national promise—begins to be applied to the just man, the saint, as in Isa. 57:13b; 65:13–16. The Wisdom literature, on the one hand, has, as we should now put it, a curiously "international" flavour (and, indeed, draws upon Egyptian and other non-Jewish sources). On the other hand, it applies appeals and warnings uttered by the prophets of Israel to the individual Israelite. It is not only that the fate of the individual is bound up with that of his people, but that the experience of Israel, as a people, is reproduced, on an appropriate scale, in that of the individual Israelite (see Prov. 1:24–28).[7]

Later still, in the Maccabean period, the martyrs further imprinted the significance of the individual Israelite on Judaism. The martyrs in the Book of Daniel and elsewhere stand to the majority of their own people, whom they regarded as "apostates," in a relationship comparable to that in which Israel as a whole had often been thought to stand to the Gentile nations. The singularity of the people of Israel in the midst of the nations is now experienced by the martyr in the midst of Israel. The triumph of the individual martyr demanded the doctrine of the resurrection of the dead. Here, as in every sphere, Judaism preserved both a communal and an individual emphasis (see Wisd. Sol. 5:1–2, which describes the triumph of the righteous in the resurrection and the discomfiture of the wicked). But the individualization and internationalization of religious con-

7. Cf. Isa. 65:2, 12; 66:4 with Prov. 1:24; Isa. 66:4 with Prov. 1:26b; Isa. 64:13–14 with Prov. 1:27c; Isa. 65:24 with Prov. 1:28. On the relation between individualism and disconnection from immediate surroundings, as in exile, see the quotation from A. N. Whitehead in *GL*, pp. 218–19. The former is often born out of the latter.

cern could not but lead to a relocation of emphasis. And this was furthered by the influence of the Dispersion or, more accurately, of the Exile.

(g) As indicated in both Hellenistic and Palestinian sources, The Land became, in some quarters, a symbol for a transcendent order, or for the age to come. Such sources can be divided into two kinds: those in which The Land retains its geographic dimension and yet is given a moral and transcendental connotation (Philo's works and a section in the Mishnah) and those in which The Land is wholly transcendentalized (the Testament of Job).

Philo hoped for a restoration to The Land in the messianic age, but the emphasis in his thought is not on The Land. In the messianic age, other nations will enjoy their own lands: what Philo is concerned with is that they should recognize and accept the Law. It is in its possession of the latter that the peculiarity of the people of Israel lies, not in its connection with The Land (Philo *Moses* 1.279). Similarly, Philo recognized that the root of anti-Judaism lay in the laws observed by his people.

Moreover, although Philo retains the actuality of the messianic hope for The Land, he can also interpret The Land symbolically. In his *Questions on Genesis,* he does not deal directly with Gen. 12:1–3, but does offer comments on Gen. 15:7, 8. In these, the promised Land becomes "fruitful wisdom." (See also Philo's comment on Gen. 15:18–21.) It does not come as a surprise, therefore, when we find The Land spiritualized in Pharisaism itself. In Mishnah Sanhedrin 10:1, we read: "All Israelites have a share in the world to come, for it is written, Thy people also shall be all righteous, they shall inherit the land for ever; the branch of my planting, the work of my hands that I may be glorified" (Isa. 60:21). To "inherit the land" is equated with having a share in "the world to come." The phrase "the world to come" may sometimes be equated with the messianic age. Here, however, the context makes it clear that it refers to the final age beyond the resurrection of the dead. The Land is no longer territorial: it has become a symbol of the life of the age to come, what the Fourth Gospel refers to as "eternal life." This symbolism appears with a different connotation in the *gemara* on M. Sanhedrin 10:3, where The Land is interpreted not as Palestine, but as "this world," and where the holy mount of Jerusalem is the equivalent of the future world, the age to come. (See also *BT* Sanhedrin 110b.)

The Land seems to be wholly transcendentalized in the little noticed and examined Testament of Job, which Kohler traced to pre-Christian Essene circles, finding its eschatology and messianic belief to be Jewish.[8] It is difficult to agree with Kohler's understanding of the eschatology. The traditional eschatological terms—throne, kingdom, glory—do appear, but the hope expressed in the Testament of Job suggests more the immortal world of souls than the resurrection of the dead. Job looks forward to an eternal order, beyond this world, where he and his children will enter into glory. In one manuscript—probably the most authentic—this eternal order is described as "the holy land," a term used in parallelism with "the imperishable world" (see Test. Job 33).

The same anticipation of a life in a world to come emerges in Job's reaction to the request of his wife, Sitis, that the bones of his children be disinterred and rendered proper, decent burial. Job's words, when the kings gave order that this should be done, are:

8. K. Kohler, "The Testament of Job."

Do not go into the trouble in vain, for
you will not find my children,
since they have been taken up into
[the] heavens by their lord and king (Test. Job 39).

On the protest of his friends, Job replied:

"Raise me that I may stand." And they raised me,
lifting up my arms on both sides. Then
standing I made confession to the Father:
And after my prayer I said to them:
"Look up with your eyes to the east and
see my children crowned alongside
the glory of the Heavenly One."

And the reaction of Sitis was to fall on the ground and exclaim: "Now I have known that the memory of me remains with the Lord." That Sitis died without proper burial (a greatly emphasized aspect of Judaism) is of no consequence: she is remembered by God. So, too, Job, who had set his hope, not on earthly things and an unstable earth, but on the living God, was not concerned to hand on to his daughters earthly or worldly well-being, and so gave them "three-stringed girdles" which transformed their existence from the earthly to the heavenly. And the worst fate that can befall Elihu, as all men, is that he should not be remembered by God or His holy ones or by the living. The reality of the supernal world is the ground of all hope and the reality of God's remembrance of us in that world.

All this is set in a discussion between Job and his friends, and they regard him as mad. Doubtless we hear the echo here of the way in which Sadducees and Samaritans, and perhaps even Pharisees, responded to those who were openly receptive to Hellenistic ideas and prepared to mythologize "The Land" or to turn it into a symbol of the transcendental. This process has been also traced in the

Book of Wisdom and in 4 Maccabees (see Wis. 3:1–4; 4 Macc. 9:21 f.).

And there is another development in the first century and later which has a bearing on our theme. It cannot be sufficiently emphasized that in Judaism two entities were indissolubly linked to The Land: Jerusalem and the Temple. But during the first century and later there was more and more concentration on the transcendental heavenly Jerusalem and heavenly Temple, whose origins are much earlier than those of their earthly analogues. Along with this, in the eschatological thinking of Judaism, there persisted the expectation of a new creation. This development—that is, the spiritualization and transcendentalizing of The Land in terms of the heavenly Jerusalem and the heavenly Temple against the background of a new creation—raises acutely the question of how far in the course of time the expectations engendered by the promise to Abraham were so transmuted that the hope of occupying The Land in history became a hope for an order beyond history. How far did The Land become a symbol for a transcendent order, the promise of territory being absorbed, and thereby annulled, in the yearning for the future "age to come" and "new creation"?

In the postexilic period, the life of Jewry was mainly centred in Jerusalem and in the area surrounding it, so that it was probably inevitable that the city should gather to itself the hopes of Israel. Geographic actualities demanded this, but it was even more rooted in the history and religion of Israel.

Pre-Israelite Jerusalem need not concern us, and a detailed account of the development of the mystique of Jerusalem in the Tanak would take us too far afield. Suffice it to say that the city became the political and religious centre of Israel in the reign of David, who introduced the Ark, the symbol of Yahweh's presence, into it. A covenant—the covenant at Sinai, adapted to changing circumstances—was formed between Yahweh and David. Through the latter, Jerusalem became the political centre of the people of God; through the Ark, the religious and historical traditions of that people were preserved and grafted on to Jerusalem, as their repository. That the traditions referred to were focused in the Ark in part explains why the prophet Nathan opposed the building of a temple. But although the spiritual centrality of Jerusalem for Israel was thus originally conditioned by the presence of the Ark within its walls, in Solomon's reign a temple was built there. This was acceptable to Yahweh, the God of Sinai, as a fit abode for his glory, and served, therefore, to increase still further the religious significance of the city.

This significance survived events which might be expected to have diminished it. It survived the division of the kingdom (Jer. 41:5); it survived the decline of the dynasty of David; it even survived the loss of the Temple and of the Ark in 587 B.C.E. Why? Although the preexilic prophets had linked Jerusalem to the dynasty of David, they had preferred, like the psalmists, to think of the city not as the city of David, but as that of Yahweh: they referred to it as Zion, the archaic name of the Jebusite acropolis that had *become* the city of David (2 Sam. 5:7). It is, therefore, not altogether surprising that the fall of the Davidic dynasty did not loosen the religious hold of the city. And although no preexilic prophet states that Yahweh had chosen Jerusalem, Isa. 14:32 does assert that He had founded it (and so was its creator). There, in the Temple, Yahweh dwelt (Amos 1:2; Isa. 2:2; 8:18; 31:9), seated on his throne, the Ark (Isa. 6:1; cf. 1 Sam. 4:4; 2 Sam. 6:2). The destruction of the Temple and the disappearance of the Ark could not but, therefore, have been traumatic experiences for the people of God. And yet Jerusalem remained its religious centre. How could this be?

It could be only because, as Jeremiah and Ezekiel make clear, apart from the Ark and the Temple, Jerusalem itself was believed to be peculiarly related to Yahweh. Jeremiah envisages the whole of Jerusalem as the throne of Yahweh in the future; he mentions no temple. In Jer. 3:16–17, Yahweh's presence, it is implied, has become independent of the Temple, as of the Ark. This divorce of Yahweh from "holy space," centered in the Temple, is evident also when we compare Isa. 2:2 with Isa. 27:13 and 66:20. The "mountain of the Lord's house" of the first passage has in both the latter become simply "the holy mountain of Yahweh." True, Ezekiel and Zechariah do see a temple in the future restored Jerusalem. But for Ezekiel, at least, the heart of that city is the presence of Yahweh himself. Its name will be : "Yahweh is there" (Ezek. 48:38). Ark and Temple might pass away, but the presence of Yahweh in the city is still assured.

But for Israel, the year 587 B.C.E. was traumatic in another way. Jerusalem itself was then reduced to ruins. This event was traumatic because of the belief that the city, as the city of Yahweh, was inviolable. The origins of this belief need not detain us. Isaiah and the Psalms point to it. Though Isaiah did not wholly endorse it, and Micah and Jeremiah rejected it, its reality for the majority of Israel cannot be doubted (Lam. 4:12; 3:31–33). (See further Ezek. 43:1–5; Deut.-Isa. 40:1–2; 49:16; 52:1; 52:8.) Yahweh cannot forget Jerusalem: "Behold, I have graven you on the palm of my hands, your walls are continually before me" (Isa. 49:16). Deutero-Isaiah pictures the dispersed Jews from many lands returning to the city (40:11; 41:17 ff.; 43:5 f.). Jerusalem will be greatly enlarged and exceedingly beautiful (49:19 ff.; 54:1–3, 11–12; 60:13–18). Haggai asserts that, "The latter splendour of this house [the rebuilt Temple] shall be greater than the former, says the Lord of hosts" (Hag. 2:9). Zechariah is assured that Yahweh "will again choose Jerusalem" (2:12; see also 1:14b, 17: 3:2) and describes the future glories of that city (8:3–8). The nations will flow to a city rebuilt and elevated miraculously above the earth (14:10 ff.). The hope for such a city in the future reaches full tide in Isa. 60–62.

The promise of a new earthly Jerusalem is stressed in many sources. We cannot pursue the evidence in detail; suffice it to refer to Tobit (ca. 200 B.C.E.), where in 1:4 we read that Jerusalem is "Chosen from among all the tribes of Israel, where all the tribes should sacrifice and where the temple of the dwelling of the Most High was consecrated and established for all generations for ever." Cf. Ecclus. 36:11–14; 51:12 (ca. 180 B.C.E.); Ps. Sol. 17:22 f. (ca. 70–40 B.C.E.); Sib. Or., passim (ca. 140 B.C.E.–C.E. 70); Test. Levi 10:5. In 3 Macc. 2:9–10 (first century B.C.E.) Jerusalem is elect from creation; in 4 Ezra (first century C.E.) it is connected with the election of the people of Israel itself (4 Ezra 5:24 ff.); cf. Num. 3:2. In Pharisaic sources, the hope for the restoration and the glorification of Jerusalem is vivid. Written well before C.E. 70, the 14th Benediction in the Shemoneh Esreh, cited above, makes this clear. (See further *BT* Megillah 17b–18a, and especially Aboth de Rabbi Nathan 35.) While the earthly Jerusalem stood, and after it had again fallen in C.E. 70, the hope for a New Jerusalem persisted.

The city had been connected with Mt. Sinai in Isa. 2:1–5. The same connection occurs in Ps. 68:15–17. But these two passages also connect Jerusalem with a conception found in Canaanite mythology—that of the mountains of the gods, of which Bashan and Zaphon and the north (Isa. 14:12–13) are examples. There is a reference to Bashan as envious of Mt. Zion in Ps. 68:15–17, but in Ps. 48:1–3 Zion is identified with Mt. Zaphon. Jerusalem has become the place of the highest mountain. The view reemerges in Ezek. 20:40; 40:2. In the latter passage, the prophet sees the future Jerusalem opposite "a very high mountain" in The Land of Israel.

The theme of the mountain reemerges in a group of psalms which are preoccupied with Zion (the psalms of Korah, 42–49; 84–85; 86–88). According to the authors of these, Yahweh dwelt exclusively in Zion. There was the house and dwelling place of God (42:4); from "the holy hill" came forth the light and truth of God (43:3). The mountain of God is mentioned in 48:2; 87:1. With this mythological motif are combined those of paradise (46:4) and of the conflict with chaos (46:2 ff.). The city is endowed with the riches of mythology to give it a cosmic significance. No wonder that those born in Jerusalem are especially blessed (Ps. 87:5). A day in the courts of her temples is better than a thousand elsewhere (Ps.84:10).

One of the most direct testimonies to the continuing vitality of the veneration of Jerusalem appears at column 22 in *IIQPs^a*, a document discovered at Qumran. The literary affinities between this column, generally referred to as the Apostrophe to Zion, and Isa. 54:60–62; 66, and other passages in the Tanak, have been pointed out. It has also been suggested that we have here a distinct stage in the theology of Zion—the application to the city of terms usually applied to God Himself: the glorification of Zion could hardly go further!

In the passages hitherto appealed to, it would seem that Jerusalem is still *in* The Land, but so transformed and idealized that it must be asked whether it is still *of* The Land. This question is especially posed by the section in Isa.

60–62, in which we claimed above that the hope for Jerusalem had reached full tide. Does it warrant the view that,
already in the Tanak, the city has become a transcendental
entity, "mystic, wonderful," so that the earthly Jerusalem
is subsumed in a heavenly city? R. de Vaux does not hesitate to claim that in Isa. 60–62 the dazzling description of
the city "has no longer any connection with earthly realities: Jerusalem transcends history; in her is summed up the
whole history of salvation."[9] Although in most of Isa.
60–62 the earthly city is surely envisaged, in Isa. 60:14–20
at least, we are pointed beyond the boundaries of time and
space. But not all have found a transcendent reference here.
The above passage may be taken as only metaphorical, and
there are certainly mundane verses in Isa. 60 in which Jerusalem is envisaged as a very earthly city, to which the
wealth of the nations is brought (Isa. 60:3, 5 ff., 10, 13).

   If we reject the view that the belief in a heavenly Jerusalem is already present in Isa. 60:19–20, it probably first
occurs in 1 Enoch 90:28–38, where, although the express
phrase "heavenly Jerusalem" does not occur, its existence is
presupposed. Here the "new house" is implied to already
exist before it is set up in what 1 Enoch 90:20 calls "the
pleasant land." It is conceived in very enlarged proportions
to contain those beasts and birds—the dispersed and
apostates—who desire to enter it. But the meaning of "new
house" is ambiguous. Usually it has been taken, without
discussion, to refer to the new Jerusalem; but it might be
interpreted as the new Temple. This ambiguity of interpretation suggests what is frequently found in the sources,
and is illustrated in quotations which follow—the interpenetration or the identification of the city and the Temple,
and the indiscriminate transition from the one to the other.
However, the magnitude of the "new house" contemplated

   9. R. de Vaux, "Jerusalem and the Prophets," p. 296.

suggests that the whole city, not merely the Temple, is in view, so that we may, though not with complete certainty, find an implicit reference here to a heavenly Jerusalem. But notice: this heavenly Jerusalem is to come down to The Land. It does not remain "in heaven": however, "heavenly," it is to become earthly.

A more unambiguous reference to a preexistent city appears in the Syriac Baruch (2 Bar.) at 4:1–7. Probably written within forty years of the destruction of the second Temple in C.E. 70, and purporting to deal with visions of destruction of the first Temple and the city in the time of Jeremiah, this work makes a clear distinction between the earthly temple and another. Here again we note the transition, without warning, from the city to the Temple. The city, no less than the Temple, existed before creation: a vision of it was granted to Adam, but withdrawn after the Fall, only to be renewed to Abraham, the father of the eschatological faith of Israel, and later to Moses. The vision of the city is granted to Abraham "by night among the portions of the victims." The reference is to Gen. 15:9–21. A vision of the city—not referred to in that text—is mentioned rather than the promise of The Land: has it taken the place of the latter in the author's mind?

The same belief in a "heavenly Jerusalem" emerges in 4 Ezra, also written after C.E. 70. Most interesting here is that the city and The Land are placed in parallelism and, thereby, perhaps equated (4 Ezra 7:26). This explains, perhaps, why in 3:13, 14 the promise of The Land to Abraham is not mentioned, but is subsumed under his vision of "the end of the times." Among the future glories of the redeemed, there is no mention of the Land, but there is of the city. 4 Ezra 8:52–53 asserts of the seer, who is among the saved:

> For you
> is opened Paradise,

> planted the Tree of Life;
> the future age prepared,
> plenteousness made ready;
> a city builded . . .
> and in the end the treaures of immortality
> are made manifest.

This passage is significant. Here, unmistakably, the "city builded" is classified with a future order which wholly transcends the historical one.

But no passage makes the existence of a heavenly Jerusalem—the city of 4 Ezra 8:52–53—clearer than the tantalizing section dealing with "The Vision of the Disconsolate Woman" in 4 Ezra 9:38–10:57. Here, despite the complexities of the text, the distinction between the earthly Jerusalem (the Son) and "the (heavenly) pattern of her" (the woman) is unmistakable. The "wholly other" character of the heavenly pattern is emphasized, especially in the section which explains why the vision had only been granted in a field: it had to be placed in a fresh setting. How important the vision of the heavenly city was for the author of 4 Ezra appears from the frequency with which he refers to it (see 7:26; 13:35 f.).

In the rabbinic sources, discussion of the heavenly Jerusalem centres on two themes. First, its exact location in the heavens—for example, is it in the third heaven or the fourth? Apart from the materials to which we have referred, the New Testament also, for example, at Rev. 21:2, 10, makes it clear that such speculation prevailed in the first century, although most of the rabbinic material dealing with it is of late origin. One text, Gen. Rabbah 69:7, places the heavenly Jerusalem eighteen miles above the earthly (so Simeon ben Yoḥai, C.E. 140–65). The same rabbi in Gen. Rabbah 55:7, on Gen. 22:2, finds that, on earth, Moriah corresponds to the heavenly Temple. In *BT* Ḥagigah 12b,

Resh Lakish (Rabbi Simeon b. Lakish, C.E. 279–320) thinks that the heavenly Temple is situated in *z'bûl* (the fourth of the seven heavens). (*Z'bûl* is that in which "[the heavenly] Jerusalem and the Temple and the altar are built, and Michael, the great prince, stands and offers up thereon an offering"; reference is made to 1 Kings 8:13 and Isa. 43:15, where *z'bûl* is referred to to as the habitation of God.) Secondly, how was this heavenly city to be made manifest? There is a sharp division between the earlier rabbinic sources and the later at this point. That there was a correspondence between the structure of the heavenly Jerusalem and the earthly was generally recognized. But none of the earlier texts suggests that the heavenly Jerusalem will descend to earth to replace the earthly: the heavenly city remains transcendent. The descent of the city envisaged in the Pseudepigrapha, referred to above, seems to be rejected. The Jerusalem on earth will be rebuilt with human hands; the heavenly Jerusalem remains above. But the two cities are connected, as in *BT* Taanith 5a. The argument here is that the words *shehûb'rah* (joined, compacted), implies that Jerusalem has a *h'bûrâh* (companion) in heaven: both earthly city and heavenly prototype are located opposite each other. And again in Mekilta, Beshallah, the assumption seems to be that "Jerusalem" existed at the time of the Exodus. Since the Jerusalem on earth did not then exist, the reference must be to the heavenly Jerusalem. A preexistent heavenly Jerusalem seems also to be implied elsewhere in the same passage: "Israel" and "Jerusalem" seem to be regarded as having been designated to be in the presence of God "from the time of the six days of creation." According to R. Eliezar Jacob, a contemporary of the destruction of C.E. 70, "Jerusalem is destined to keep rising aloft until it reaches the throne of glory" (Pesikta de Rab Kahana, end of section 20). Does this mean that the earthly

Jerusalem is ultimately to be united with the heavenly one—that is, to become wholly transcendent—or simply that there is no fundamental difference between the earthly and the heavenly Jerusalem? This question must remain unanswered. Was Philo of Alexandria's understanding of the tabernacle built by Moses that it only *resembled* its heavenly prototype (*Moses* 11.74 ff.)? "The tabernacle, then, was constructed to resemble a sacred temple in the way described," we are told (*Moses* 11.59). How much beyond Philo the rabbis went in connecting the earthly and the heavenly city remains problematic.

At no point should the doctrine of the promise of The Land be separated from that of Yahweh as Creator of the universe. And, in the eschatology of Israel, that promise must more and more be understood in a larger context, against the eschatological doctrine of a new creation. Only the bare structure of this doctrine need be given here. Already in Isa. 11:6, a passage usually referred to as messianic, the end is conceived of as the restoration of the beginning: a return to the paradisal conditions existing before the fall of Adam. By the time of Trito-Isaiah, the belief that cosmic changes will mark the end becomes explicit: "For, behold, I create new heavens and a new earth" (Isa. 65:17). There are parallels in both Isa. 66:22 and Deut.-Isa. 51:6, the latter passage contrasting this passing material world with God's salvation, which is to be for ever.

Later sources reveal a bewildering variety of views on the end: in most, it will be by fire, the final destruction by fire corresponding to the initial destruction by the flood; it will occur sometime after the messianic age, or before the final judgment of God. If there is to be a "place" for salvation, where is that to be, in heaven or on earth after it has been scorched? What is meant by the "new heaven"? Is the old earth to be undone and then remade out of a new sub-

stance? Or is the earth in its present material form to un-
dergo a transformation? Or is it, without undergoing dissolution, to be purified? Or is "the new" to be wholly
unrelated to the old? Such questions are reflected in the
Apocrypha and Pseudepigrapha, the Qumran writings,
and the rabbinic sources. And speculation about the end
also occurs in another frame of reference, in Hellenistic
sources, which also reveal that the future may lead to a fiery
end of all things.

The promise of The Land, cherished as we have seen it
to be, must be considered in the framework of such speculation, which could not but have depressed the doctrine of
The Land to a less central position than it would otherwise
have occupied. The flames of the end, feeding on a cosmos
afire, would tend to diminish interest in The Land as such.

EXILE AND DISPERSION

In the preceding section, historical and theological data
from the Tanak and later sources were presented which
inhibit the simplistic ascription of a single territorial doctrine to Judaism. We now turn to another very critical
aspect of Jewish history which militates against any uncritical elevation of The Land in Judaism. The condition
and distribution of Jews outside The Land in the postexilic
period deserves attention. Few of the exiles in Babylon
chose to return to The Land when Cyrus (B.C.E. 538) made
this possible. For a thousand years after Cyrus, there continued in Babylon a well-organized Jewish community,
which eventually gave the Babylonian Talmud to the
world. The Jews had early spread to the west also. As is
made clear in the Elephantine papyrii, there was a colony
of Jewish soldiers in the city of Yeb (Elephantine) in Egypt
at the beginning of the sixth century B.C.E.. Alexander the
Great stimulated the spread of Jews, and throughout the

Greek and Roman periods various reasons contributed to
further this. Already around 168–65 B.C.E., the Jews had
built a temple at Leontopolis in Egypt, in which they had
offered sacrifices. Although in contravention of the Torah,
the sages in Palestine seem to have accepted this. Jews in
Sardis in Asia Minor under John Hyrcanus II established
their own cult (Josephus *Antiquities* 14. 10. 24). Josephus
quotes Strabo, the geographer (ca. 40 B.C.E.–C.E. 24):
"This people has already made its way into every city, and
it is not that easy to find any place in the habitable world
which has not received this nation and in which it has not
made its power felt" (*Ant.* 14. 7.2). Few have written as
perceptively on this dispersion as Bickerman, who notes
the continued attachment of the Diaspora Jews to Jerusalem:

The post-biblical period of Jewish history [that is, that following
Nehemiah] . . . is marked by a unique and rewarding polarity: on
the one hand, the Jerusalem center and, on the other, the plurality
of centers in the Diaspora. The Dispersion saved Judaism from
physical extirpation and spiritual inbreeding. Palestine united the
dispersed members of the nation and gave them a sense of one-
ness. This counterpoise of historical forces is without analogy in
antiquity. . . . The Jewish Dispersion continued to consider Jerusalem as the "metropolis" (Philo), turned to the Holy Land for
guidance, and in turn, determined the destinies of its inhabitants.[10]

But the experience of living outside The Land could not
but tend to detach Jews from it. In this sphere, as in others,
absence made the heart grow fonder, but the Babylonian
exiles chose not to return to The Land, and those at Leontopolis were apparently content to be settled there. Later,

10. E. Bickerman, *From Ezra to the Last of the Maccabees*,
pp. 3 f.

the Jews of Alexandria opposed the Sicarii,[11] and the Dispersion everywhere on the whole refused to cooperate in the war against Rome in C.E. 66–70. They had their own life to live outside The Land, and a form of religious association appropriate for such a life, the synagogue, had already almost certainly emerged, if not in the Babylonian exile, at least by the third century B.C.E., and developed throughout the dispersion to supply Jews with a rallying point other than the Jerusalem Temple. In time, the dispersion, which had been regarded as a punishment for sin, could be justified by at least two rabbis. Rabbi Eleazer of Modiim (C.E. 120–40) said that "God scattered Israel among the nations for the sole end that proselytes should wax numerous among them." And although his was apparently a lonely voice, it is not without significance: separation from The Land could be regarded as a not unmitigated evil. Philo came to regard the dispersion as under the providence of God (*Flaccus* 45). In the late Middle Ages, the Lurianic Qabbala came to give a profound meaning to the Exile of the Jewish people, which it explained in subtle mythical terms.

Vital rightly notes that "exile" has been the distinctive characteristic of Jewish life.[12] It has been ineluctable and extraordinarily rich and creative in Jewish history. Certain historical facts are fundamental. The Land of Israel was not the birthplace of the Jewish people, which did not emerge there (as most peoples have on their own soil). On the contrary it had to enter its own Land from without; there is a sense in which Israel was born in exile. Abraham had to leave his own land to go to the Promised Land: the father of Jewry was deterritorialized. Paradoxically, on reaching

11. Philo Judaeus, *Embassy to Gaius.*
12. D. Vital, *The Origins of Zionism,* p. 1.

The Land, he did not possess it; he roamed in it and dug wells. He did not chase the Canaanites out of it. On discovering that The Land could not maintain them both, he divided it with his cousin Lot (Gen. 13:6). That is, there was a "territorial concession" on his part. According to some, so little did Abraham "possess" The Land that he had to "buy" a grave for his wife at Machpelah.[13]

As for the spiritual history of Jews, its heroic periods have often been outside The Land. The Torah itself, the heart of Judaism as we shall urge, was given outside The Land, in the desert, in "no-man's-land," at Mount Sinai. Much of the Tanak, and the Talmud itself in its Babylonian form, were redacted outside The Land. It is surprising that, until late in the Middle Ages, Judaism did not produce a developed theology of exile (although such a theology can be extracted from Jeremiah and Ezekiel, as T. M. Raitt has shown in his recent study of these prophets).

The fact that since the Babylonian Exile there have almost certainly been more Jews outside than in The Land, so that even today Israelis are only a fraction of world Jewry, cannot but have diminished the centrality of The Land among many Jews and influenced their attitudes towards the doctrine concerning it. The prominence of the state of Israel in our time can easily hide the significance of the Exile for Judaism throughout most of its history. But the theological preeminence in Jewish history of Jews outside The Land needs no documentation. Apart from all else, their significance in the very survival of Judaism must be recognized. The loss of the Temple and The Land, the

13. See J. W. Bowman, *Which Jesus?* p. 68. Bowman's appendix 4, "Did God Give the Holy Land to Abram and His Descendants" pp. 166–68, deserves serious attention, but we are not convinced that his interpretation of Gen. 23 is to be followed. For another interpretation of this purchase, see *GL*, p. 222, n. 17.

centres of Judaism, could be sustained only because there were organized Jewish communities scattered elsewhere. Disaster at the centre did not spell the end of Judaism but could be, and was, offset and cushioned by its existence elsewhere. From this point of view, exile may be regarded as having been the historical condition for the survival of Judaism and Jewry. (That this did not mean a radical decline of the significance of the primary centre we shall show later.)

Such considerations explain the long discussion on the role of Exile and Diaspora among Jews. There have always been large number of Jews in the Diaspora who have accepted the territorial doctrine as such. The literal acceptance of the doctrine is best exemplified, perhaps, in Sabbatianism and among those Jews who settled in Palestine long before the emergence of the state of Israel. For reasons previously elaborated, Zionism cannot be equated with a reaffirmation of the eternal relation of The Land, the people, and the Deity, except with the most cautious reservations, since it is more the expression of nationalism than of Judaism. But many Jews in the Diaspora have sought other ways to deal with the particularity of The Land. Some insist that The Land is still *central* for Judaism but not *primary*; others in the Diaspora express the matter in terms of *centre* and *periphery*, or of an ellipse with two poles, claiming that The Land is not always necessarily central. At first encounter, such views appear merely face-saving: certainly the distinction between the central and the primary, it might be argued, is a distinction without a difference. Is it not simply a tacit admission that the doctrinal claims for The Land have become an embarrassment? In fact, the view is another expression of a prolonged concern in the Diaspora to transcend the theological distinction between Palestinian and Diaspora Judaism, and to find a raison d'être for the Diaspora which gives it that significance which its dominating actuality seems to demand. In modern times, these views are associated with such names as Moses Mendelssohn (1729–86), Samuel Holdheim (1806–60), Abraham Geiger (1810–74), and Hermann Cohen (1842– 1918). The attitude to which we refer gives to the Diaspora (not here understood as "exile") an independent spiritual raison d'être, and finds in it the very self-fulfillment of Judaism. This theology of the Diaspora has been summarized by André Neher as follows:

The *Shekinah* resides with every exiled fragment of the Jewish people. In every particle of land trodden by a Jew the presence of God is revealed. Far from being an outward road leading the chosen People farther and farther away from their election, the exile is for Israel a mission, each stage of which strengthens the bonds between the Jew and the God who accompanies him. . . . The universe would be lacking in shape unless Israel were omnipresent, making the divine sap pulsate through the organism of the cosmos like the blood through the body. . . . In each field of his exile the Jew places the seeds which will one day bring forth the divine harvest.[14]

In order to justify the claim of an independent religious viability and dignity for the Diaspora, appeal has been

14. Cited in 'Abd Al-Tafāhum, "Doctrine," p. 374, from Neher's *Moses and the Vocation of the Jewish People*, p. 162. 'Abd Al-Tafāhum also refers to the views of Franz Rosenzweig and Hans Joachim Schoeps, but these are not directly related to the question of The Land by him. See, however, T. Dreyfus, "The Commentary of Franz Rosenzweig to the Poems of Jehudah Halevi." For the notions of centre and periphery and of Jewish existence as an ellipse between Jerusalem and Babylon or Russia and America, etc., see P. Nave, "Zentrum und Peripherie im Geschichte und Gegenwart." On "the mission of Israel," see also J. J. Petuchowski, *Zion Reconsidered*, pp. 120–23.

made not only to the theology described by Neher, but to history. Emphasis is laid on the fact that the Diaspora was born as much out of deliberate departures from The Land as out of necessity—through wars, enslavement, expulsion. Largely voluntary, the Diaspora was well established before the tragic events of the first century C.E., and must not be regarded as predominantly a consequence of these. Outside The Land, Jews have developed a religious life of their own, respecting the authorities of The Land, but not dominated by them. As indicated before, rabbinic Judaism recognized a distinction between commandments which only could be, and had to be, practised in The Land and those which could and had to be practised outside The Land. The logical outcome of this was that in time it came to be affirmed that the Jews were religiously bound to abide by the civil law of the countries where they dwelt. To what degree and how long Palestinian authorities controlled the Diaspora after 70 C.E. is a matter of debate. E. E. Urbach has dealt with this problem in terms of the relation between The Land as centre and the Diaspora as periphery. After a survey of various treatments of the theme, and an illuminating examination of the evidence from the period of the second Temple and the centuries following its destruction, he concludes that without the precondition of Jewish sovereignty and independence in The Land, "any attempt to prove its continuance as a Jewish center cannot succeed, and all concepts of center and dispersion in Jewish history are merely reconstructions without basis in fact."[15] For him only the self-determination of the Jewish people in its own Land could and can make The Land the centre of Jewish existence. Certainly after the period to which Urbach ap-

15. E. E. Urbach, "Center and Periphery in Jewish Historic Consciousness."

peals, many Jews, religious as well as secular, have come to regard the Diaspora as capable of maintaining an authentic Jewish way of life in any locality and independently of any central authority in The Land. Theological considerations have given way to historical actualities and necessities.

And this adaptation has been justified by a second historical consideration. A doctrine that was theologically and socially appropriate immediately after the collapse of the revolt in the late first century, and even for the greater Diaspora which developed after 70 C.E., it is implied, cannot reasonably be expected to be uncritically endorsed after twenty centuries of growth of the Diaspora throughout the world. After so many centuries of life outside The Land, religiously, culturally, and otherwise, most Diaspora Jews would find such an endorsement hard to support. Not only have time and change taught them new duties, but the undeniable creativity of Diaspora Jews, religiously as well as otherwise, makes their claim to authentic Jewish existence impossible to ignore, and any uncritical acceptance of the continuance of The Land as *the* Jewish centre unrealistic. After the Six Day War of 1967, the claims of The Land came to be felt with renewed force. A Jewish scholar, asking what attitude Jews should take to The Land, could nonetheless express the view that, while taking note of the existence of the state of Israel as a country largely inhabited by Jews, the Diaspora should "then proceed with the business in hand." It might recognize the state of Israel as Judaism's "show case" to the world at large, but it would also maintain that Judaism has become sufficiently independent of geography so that the Jewish religious problems of New York and of London can be, and have to be, settled in New York and London—and not in Tel Aviv or Jerusalem. There can be a "full-blooded Judaism which is in no need to hope and to pray for a messianic return to Palestine."[16]

For E. E. Urbach, only an independent sovereign Jewish state in The Land can make of The Land the centre; for J. J. Petuchowski, under the present significant preponderance of the Diaspora, even such a state cannot justify this. For Urbach, the centrality of The Land depends upon its independent political vitality; for Petuchowski, the Jewish existence outside The Land already has such vitality that it can relegate The Land to secondary—even insignificant —status. But on one very significant point both scholars are alike. They make no reference in their conclusions to the territorial theological tradition with which we have here been concerned. If we understand him aright, Urbach conditions even the significance of The Land, primarily at least, on its political power. As for Petuchowski's view, it seems virtually to reduce the suggested distinction between a central and a primary role for The Land to a triviality, and the momentous efforts of many Jews to achieve a life in The Land to a "show case to the world at large."[17] The doctrine of The Land, so tenaciously held across centuries and at such cost, seems to end, for the one scholar, in realpolitik, and for the other in a worthy advertisement. However, such a statement does not do justice especially to Urbach's view or the several treatments of the question elsewhere, as U. Tal makes clear in "The Land and the State of Israel in Israeli Religious Life." Both Urbach and Petuchowski, moreover, reveal the pressure to come to terms with the actuality of the Diaspora, movingly expressed—as is the mystique of The Land—in words

16. J. J. Petuchowski, "Diaspora Judaism—An Abnormality?" p. 27.

17. Petuchowski, *Zion Reconsidered*, p. 132.

penned in New York city, *centrum mundi*, by Dr. Louis Finkelstein, in a description of his understanding of his own work:

> We at the Seminary regard ourselves and American Jewry nei-
> ther as one of the foci of a great ellipse nor the center of a circle
> with only mystic connections with a similar circle surrounding
> Jerusalem. We recognize that we stand on the periphery of Jewish
> inspiration; and if we are content with our position, it is only
> because we believe that the service we can render God, Torah, and
> mankind from this stance is one to which we have been called and
> which we cannot neglect. Yet always we turn to Zion not only in
> prayer but also in the hope of instruction. We gladly assume the
> role of amanuensis to our brethren who have been given the
> superior privilege of serving God and studying Torah in the land
> in which both were uniquely revealed. If the experiences we have
> garnered in our efforts to weave the tapestry we have mentioned
> may prove of use, they are at the disposal of our masters and
> teachers in Israel and Zion.[18]

Not all Diaspora Jews have shared this veneration for The Land, however. Many have succumbed to one extent or another to the blandishments of life outside its borders, or come to terms with it in other ways.

THE WITNESS OF HISTORY: THE CLASSICAL RABBINIC ATTITUDE

Judaism survived and came to terms with the loss of The Land in C.E. 70, catastrophic as it was, with dignity and comparative speed. It did so because Pharisaism, after C.E. 70 the dominant element in Judaism, was politically and otherwise prepared to adjust to the absence of The Land, as to the loss of other symbols of its faith. This is not as surprising as at first encounter. The relations of the Phari-

18. L. Finkelstein, "Israel as a Spiritual Force," p. 16.

sees to the Maccabees had foreshadowed their reaction to the fall of Jerusalem. Commenting on the estrangement of the Pharisees from the Maccabean dynasty, Bickerman writes:

to them [the Pharisees] it must have appeared that a foreign domination respecting Jewish autonomy and recognizing the Torah as the binding law of Judaism would offer less hindrance to their work of education. Precisely because it was foreign, and hence concerned only for the prompt payment of tribute and for civil order, they assumed that the internal life of the people would remain outside the range of its interest.

. . . the Pharisees might justly expect foreign rulers scrupulously to follow the opinions of the scholars in all such [legal] matters whereas a Jewish King, as was the case with the Maccabees, would desire to shape even the internal and religious life of the people according to his own notions and not always according to the recommendations of the teachers of the law. In point of fact, it was the Roman rule which made possible and facilitated the development of Pharisaic Judaism to a high degree, until the great conflict between the two unequal powers set in. In this conflict the Jewish people lost its land, in order to win a historic continuity such as was vouchsafed to no other people of antiquity, not even to their conquerors, the Romans.[19]

It was the Pharisaic understanding of Judaism that made this continuity possible—an understanding that placed Torah above political power and control of The Land. That the Pharisaic position had much to support it is clear. According to the Torah itself, the possession of The Land was to be subordinated to obedience to the Torah. The promise was not of a continued possession of The Land, but of a possession conditioned by observance. Although possession of The Land had been promised, it was not neces-

19. Bickerman, *From Ezra to the Last of the Maccabees*, pp. 3 f.

sarily perdurable or without interruption. But, as a corollary, the loss of The Land did not necessarily have to
mean the end of the people. And the history of Israel had
abundantly confirmed this.

This brings us to the reorganization of Judaism by the
sages at Jamnia after the fall of Jerusalem in 70 C.E., when
they formulated the liturgy and the canon and codified the
Torah. The question is whether it was their aim and
achievement so to reinterpret Judaism that it could persist
without The Land, Jerusalem, and the Temple? Nineteenth-century scholars thought that it was. But the issue is
not to be settled so simply. The ambiguity of the rabbinic
position has to be recognized. The rabbis at Jamnia did
deliberately seek to establish a sentiment for Torah (and
ipso facto for the synagogue) which would *comfort* Israel for
its loss of The Land, the city, and the Temple. But this
sentiment for Torah was not to be a final substitute for the
latter triad. The Pharisees after 70 C.E., no less than in the
Maccabean period, were realists. In the latter period, they
came to recognize that the Maccabees would not act in
accordance with the law as they desired and therefore withdrew their support from them. In the Roman period, also,
they recognized political realities, and after 70 C.E., while
by no means abandoning ultimate hope for The Land, the
city, and the Temple, sought comfort in devotion to the
Torah, with all that this implied for their personal and
communal life. The fact that Rabbi Johanan b. Zakkai
claimed for Jamnia the prerogatives of the Temple at Jerusalem (Mishnah Rosh Hashanah 4:1; *BT* Rosh Hashanah
29b), and followed the policy of excluding former Temple
officials from authority, meant that "place" could be transcended. Some have argued that Johanan was trying to free
Judaism from connection with Jerusalem and the Temple.
But this is untenable. Johanan did not reject the Temple: he

merely sought to provide an "interim" form for religious life. (In Jewish history that interim has been variously understood as preceding a return to The Land or the end of all things.)

The passages to which appeal can be made in support of the ambiguity to which we refer are very numerous. Here we shall merely note those which indicate how the rabbis came to terms with their new situation after the fall of Jerusalem. Some denied that the Shekinah (the Divine Presence) had ever rested on the second Temple at all (Pesikta Rabbati 160a), others asserted that the Shekinah is everywhere and therefore could not be confined to the Temple, but might be present in the humblest synagogue (Exod. Rabbah 2:5; Deut. Rabbah 7:2; Lev. Rabbah 4:8; *BT* Berakoth 10a). Some claimed that mercy, and not sacrifice, was important (Aboth de Rabbi Nathan 6; Deut. Rabbah 5:3). Above all, it came to be urged that study of Torah ensures the presence of the Shekinah; it replaces sacrifice, and is more important than the rebuilding of the Temple (Mishnah Aboth 3:2; Pesikta de Rab Kahanah 60b; *BT* Megillah 16b; *BT* Shabbath 119b). Some held that "if one repents, it is imputed to him as if he had gone up to Jerusalem, built the Temple, erected an altar and offered upon it all the sacrifices enumerated in the Torah" (Lev. Rabbah 7:2).

These passages reveal that the Temple and the city—and, we may presume, The Land—could be spiritualized even while the hope for their restoration was retained. It was its ability to detach its loyalty from "place," while nonetheless retaining "place" in its memory, that enabled Pharisaism to transcend the loss of its Land. Nor was it unique in this. The same spiritualization of the *realia* of their faith had previously emerged among the sectarians at Qumran. They interpreted the community itself as the Temple: the presence of God shifted for them from a physical building to the "spiritual" domain of the community itself. The spiritualization went further. At Qumran, as in Pharisaism, obedience to the Torah became the true sacrifice of the new Temple (*IQS* 3:11–12; 4:21; 5:5 ff.; 8:4–11; 9:3–6; 4Q Flor. 1:6 f.). At the same time, as among the Pharisees, so among the sectarians, the hope for a new and restored Temple and cult at Jerusalem remained strong. Religion, like philosophy, has its antinomies and paradoxes.

In the preceding pages we have pointed to attitudes and historical realities which make it clear that there was before 70 C.E., and immediately after in the early Tannaitic period, no uniformity of territorial doctrine. And despite the overwhelming dominance of the rabbinic form of Judaism since then, the history of the Jews, although not to the same degree, reveals the same fissiparous, amorphous, and unsystematized doctrinal character. The concept of an adamant, uniform "orthodox" Judaism, which was not stirred by dissident movements and ideas or by the mystical, messianic yearnings which expressed themselves outside of, or in opposition to, the main, strictly rabbinic, tradition, is no longer tenable. To define the place of Eretz Israel in Judaism requires recognition that that place has changed—or, more accurately, has received different emphases among various groups and at different times. However persistent some views of, and attachments to, The Land have been, and however uniform the testimony of the classical sources, there has not been one unchangeable, essential doctrine universally and uniformly recognized by the whole of Judaism. In the Middle Ages, a controversy which circled around Maimonides (1135–1204) is illuminating. In his *Dalālat al-Hāʾirīn* (translated into English as *The Guide of the Perplexed*), the Great Eagle never concerned himself directly with "The Land." Although he did so in his commentary on the Mishnah, his silence about The Land in the *Guide* caused dismay and dispute among the rabbis. It led Naḥmanides (1194–1270) to criticize the Great Eagle by insisting that there was a specific *mitzwah* to settle in The Land, a *mitzwah* which Maimonides had ignored. In modern times, reform Judaism in the United States, anxious to come to terms with Western culture, has been careful to avoid any emphasis on particularistic elements in Judaism that would set Jews apart from their Christian neighbors. Until very recently, when external and internal pressures made themselves felt, the doctrine of The Land tended to be ignored or spiritualized. It was an embarrassment.

The demotion of The Land and the messianic idea, with its disturbing potentialities, was no less evident in the liberal Judaism of nineteenth-century Europe. How far the confused and confusing embarrassment with The Land went there, even among Jewish theologians, appears from Hermann Cohen. In 1880 he claimed that Judaism was already in process of forming a "cultural, historical union with Protestantism." It is not surprising that he could write:

The loss of the national state is already conditioned by messianism. But this is the basis of the tragedy of Jewish peoplehood in all historic depth. How can a people exist and fulfill its messianic task if it is deprived of the common human protection afforded by a state to its people? And yet, just this is the situation of the Jewish people, and *thus it must needs be the meaning of the history of the Jews*, if indeed this meaning lies in messianism [emphasis added].[20]

20. H. Cohen, *Die Religion der Vernunft aus den Quellen des Judentums,* pp. 311–12.

Cohen was concerned with the state and Judaism; by implication, however, he here questioned the messianic destiny
of Israel in its own Land. Even if he still recognized that
destiny as a reality, he so domesticated it in the context of
his Western Europe that it bore little resemblance to the
dynamic messianism expressed in previous Jewish history.
Cohen's "messianism" eradicated the Davidic Messiah and
the hope of a kingdom of God on earth—and with this any
hope for The Land. That reform and liberal Judaism in the
United States and Europe have recently reintroduced an
emphasis on The Land, in response to contemporary events
which they could not ignore, cannot obliterate their earlier
nonterritorial or antiterritorial attitude. Not unrelated to
this discussion in reform and liberal Judaism, though not
directly connected with those movements, is the insistence
of such figures as Aḥad Ha'Am (1856–1927) that Jews first
need to devote themselves to spiritual renewal, not to the
occupation of a territory. Aḥad Ha'Am founded a select
and secret society in 1899 "dedicated to the notion that
moral and cultural preparation had to precede the material
salvation of the Jews."[21]

All this means that, at first sight at least, the witness of
history can be taken as suggesting that Eretz Israel has not
been of the essence of Judaism to the extent that the literary
sources and liturgies and observances of pious Jews, and
even the political activity of nonreligious Jews, would seem
to suggest. Certain aspects of that history are pertinent. We
have elsewhere indicated that, although it was assumed,
there was no explicit appeal to the doctrine of The Land in
the Maccabean revolt or that against Rome in C.E. 66. This
is striking. Even more overlooked have been the protests
expressed in the Maccabean period against the Hasmonaean

21. Vital, *Origins of Zionism*, p. 156.

rulers who had created an independent state. These protests made the later attitudes of the Pharisaic leaders in coming to terms with Roman rule and in declaring the laws of The Land, wherever Jews dwelt, to be Law, less innovative than has customarily been recognized. And, at this point, the nature of the rabbinic attitude across the centuries must be fully recognized. That the doctrine of The Land remained honored among the rabbis cannot be doubted. But, despite the facts referred to in the preceding pages, after C.E. 70, and Bar Kokba and Rabbi Akiba in the second century C.E., until very recent times it was a doctrine more honoured in word than in deed. After C.E. 70, the powerlessness of Jews against the Roman authorities left the rabbinic leaders no choice other than submission and acquiescence to their divorce from "The Land." This submission and acquiescence were to persist and mold the life of the majority of Jews up to the present century and enabled the rabbis to come to terms with the loss of their Temple, city, and Land. As we have seen, protests in various forms against exile did not cease. The Lurianic Qabbalah, for example, was a magnificent attempt to confront the curse of exile, and Sabbatianism in its historical context can be regarded as a desperate lunge at the kingdom of God, which would lead to a return to Eretz Israel. But very widely, both in orthodox Judaism (by which is here meant the rabbinic mainstream) and in reform Judaism in the United States and Western Europe, the question of The Land was postponed to the age to come, either as an unacknowledged embarrassment or as a last, or ultimate, hope. Across the centuries, most Jews have lived at the whim of the Gentile world: they have not been able to afford to risk alienating their Gentile rulers by giving practical expression to their visions of a territorial return to Eretz Israel: for most Jews, despite some brilliant exceptions, such visions were a lux-

ury of Sabbath reading, dreams to be indulged in, but not
actively realized in daily life. Instead, the rabbis emphasized
that the Torah itself was to become a "portable land" for
Jews: it could be obeyed everywhere, and could and would
constitute the centre of Jewish religious identity everywhere. The Mishnah is a map without territory.[22] Generally, orthodox Judaism has refused to indulge in political

22. In "Map Without Territory," Jacob Neusner sets the Mishnaic system of sacrifice and sanctuary in its historical context.
After 70 C.E., the city of Jerusalem was in ruins; and after 135
C.E., the locus for the cult was inaccessible—the cosmic centre of
Jewry was gone. "The problem confronting all Israelites in the ten
decades from 70–170," Neusner observes, "is to work out a way
of viewing the world, of making sense of a cosmos which, having
lost its center, is nonsense" (p. 110). The sages meet this problem
by drawing up a map of a never-never land which does not and
cannot exist, a map which ignores territory. This map, the Mishnah, is a work of imagination amazingly irrelevant to its own day.
In one sense, the Mishnah is locative (see p. 121) and organizes the
world around the themes and topics of the Temple. But what does
it say to a world which cannot have a temple? The Mishnah
mediates the old world, which had the Temple, to a new world
that has none: it refers backward, but also forward—now to a
community. "Now the focus will be upon a people, not place;
anywhere, not somewhere. . . . In the world of disaster and cata-
clysmic change, Mishnah stands as a statement of how the old is
to be retained. It defines the conditions of permanence amid
change" (p. 122). "What Mishnah does by representing this cult,
laying out its measurements, describing its rite, and specifying its
rules, is to permit Israel in the words of the Mishnah to experience
anywhere and anytime that cosmic center of the world described
by Mishnah: *Cosmic center in words is made utopia*" (p. 125; italics
in original), "Mishnah is mobile. Memorizing its words is the
guarantee of ubiquity" (p. 125). Neusner rightly connects this
with the "anthropologization" of the cosmos which was taking
place at the end of the classical period. The masters of the Mishnah
are counterparts of the "holy man" who emerged at the end of the

speculation and activity which might further a return to The Land, and has accepted instead an attitude of quietism. In one of the paradoxes of history, rabbis and apocalyptists were here at one: they have preferred to wait for Divine intervention, usually postponed to an indefinite future, to produce the return. From a different point of view, as we saw, the reform, in order to accommodate its faith to the nineteenth century and to make it comparable and compatible with Christianity, also preferred to refuse to give to "The Land" a special overwhelming significance. In brief, in most rabbinic writers up to the twentieth century, and in some orthodox circles even up to the very present, the significance of The Land, though never denied, has been transferred to the "end of days." Paradoxically, "The Land" retained its geographic character and actuality, and was not always transcendentalized, although it was largely removed de facto from the realm of history altogether. In the reform, again in some circles even up to very recent times, "The Land" was conveniently relegated to a secondary place; its geographic actuality was either sublimated or transformed into a symbol of an ideal society not necessarily located in Eretz Israel. Historically then, out of necessity since C.E. 70, and Bar Kokba and Rabbi Akiba, the doctrine of The Land as a communal concern (it was often

---

classical world at the expense of the Temple. (Neusner quotes Peter Brown, *The World of Late Antiquity*, p. 102, and J. Z. Smith, *Map Is Not Territory*, on this.) Although the Mishnah never says so (p. 119), Neusner is careful to note that the hope is that the centre—the geographic centre—will once more be regained (p. 125). One might suggest that despite the suspicion of false apocalyptic hopes among the sages, hope for The Land underlay their activity. The "anthropologization" and "communalization" (to use these ugly shorthand words) were probably less conscious than Neusner's treatment allows.

cherished by individual Jews) has been largely dormant or
suffered benign neglect in much of Judaism.

What happened is apparent. In their realism, the rabbis at
Jamnia had triumphed over the Zealots of Masada. They
recognized that the power of Rome was invincible: for
them, Jewish survival lay in sensible—because unavoidable—political submission, and in obedience to the Torah
in all aspects of life where this was possible. The law of the
country where Jews dwelt became law. (The principle was
dînâ' d'malkûtâ' dîna': see *BT* Nedarim 28a; *BT* Gittin 10b;
BT Baba Kamma 113a–b; *BT* Baba Bathra 54b.) The par-
adigmatic figure was Johanan ben Zakkai, who had asked
of Vespasian only permission to found a school where he
could teach and establish a house of prayer and perform all
the commandments—a spiritual center which accepted political powerlessness. For most of the rabbis after C.E. 70,
exile became an accepted condition. For them, discretion
was the better part of valour. That it is to their discretion
that Judaism owes its existence since C.E. 70 can hardly be
gainsaid.

THE IMPACT OF ZIONISM

So far we have mainly dealt with the sources and past
history of Judaism. It is necessary to recognize, however,
that the very discussion of this theme in this volume would
probably not have been evoked were it not for the pressure,
both conscious and unconscious, of the Zionist movement.
The ascribing of a theological concern with The Land to
Jews who entertain no definable Jewish theology, or even
reject the tradition of their fathers, has become insidiously
easy because of the Zionist climate within which so much
of modern Jewry lives.

Neat dichotomies between the religious and political factors in Zionism are falsifications of their rich and mutually

accommodating diversity. To read Gershom Scholem's autobiographical pages is to be made aware of this. The Zionist movement can effectively be dated to the Congress of Basel in 1897. It grew until, after almost twenty centuries abeyance, the state of Israel emerged in 1948. But the role of Jewish territorial doctrine and sentiment in the movement has to be carefully assessed: it can easily be exaggerated. Certainly the territorial theology of Judaism should not be directly ascribed (the qualifying adverb is important) to the many nonreligious Jews who played a most significant part in Zionist history. At first it was possible for some of the leading Zionists to contemplate the establishment of a state outside The Land altogether—in Uganda, in Argentina, in newly conquered Russian territories in Asia, in Asiatic Turkey, and in North America.[23] The often silent but almost ubiquitous presence of the religious tradition, with its concentration on Eretz Israel, caused such to change their minds, however, and made the choice of the Jewish homeland inevitable. Herzl, like other Zionist secularists, was compelled to recognize this.

But Zionism remained an expression not only—and probably not even chiefly—of the theological territorial attachment of Judaism, but even more of the nationalist and socialistic spirit of the nineteenth century. In this sense, it is a typical product of that century. An examination of the history of Zionism makes its specifically religious motivation less significant than an uncritical emphasis on territorial theology would lead one to expect. In reply to an

23. The notion of "territorialism" unrelated to Eretz Israel—that is, the belief that the precise place possessed was not important, so long as Jews had a place—is associated especially with Y. L. Pinsker (1821–91), whose pamphlet *Auto-Emancipation: Mahnruf an seine Stammesgenossen von einem Russischen Juden* was published in 1892 (see Vital, *Origins of Zionism*, pp. 338–89).

article by Yeuda Bourla, a novelist who died in 1970, Gershom Scholem said:

I . . . am opposed, like thousands of other Zionists . . . to mixing up religious and political concepts. *I categorically deny that Zionism is a messianic movement and that it is entitled to use religious terminology to advance its political aims.*

The redemption of the Jewish people, which as a Zionist I desire, is in no way identical with the religious redemption I hope for the future. I am not prepared as a Zionist to satisfy political demands or yearnings that exist in a strictly nonpolitical, religious sphere, in the sphere of End-of-Days apocalyptics. The Zionist ideal is one thing and the messianic ideal is another, and the two do not touch except in pompous phraseology of mass rallies, which often fuse into our youth a spirit of new Sabbatianism that must inevitably fail. The Zionist movement is congenitally alien to the Sabbatian movement, and the attempts to infuse Sabbatian spirit into it has already caused it a great deal of harm.[24]

It seems that Scholem would here largely recognize Zionism as comparable with other nationalistic movements, such as those of Italy and many other countries in the nineteenth century. In a summary of forces which led to the triumph of Zionism, Scholem writes with greater fullness as follows:

If Zionism triumphed—at least on the level of historical decisions in the history of the Jews—it owes its victory preeminently to three factors that left their imprint on its character: it was, all in all, a movement of the young, in which strong romantic elements inevitably played a considerable role; it was a movement of social protest, which drew its inspiration as much from the primordial and still vital call of the prophets of Israel as from the slogans of European socialism; and it was prepared to identify

24. "With Gershom Scholem: An Interview," in Scholem, *Jews and Judaism in Crisis*, ed. W. J. Dannhauser, p. 44.

itself with the fate of the Jews in all—and I mean all—aspects of that fate, the religious and worldly ones in equal measure.[25]

This admirably balanced assessment is as significant for what it does not contain—i.e., apocalyptic territorial messianism—as for what it does. Scholem, while recognizing the role of the religious tradition, does not make it the dominant factor. To him Zionism was essentially a sociopolitical protest. In the judgment of many Jews, the Congress of Basel was important not primarily because it gave expression to a strictly religious hope for The Land, living and creative as that was, but to a concern for the actual economic, political, and social distress, and often despair, of Jews in Europe; it was a response not so much to a crisis in Judaism and to an endemic territorial theology as to the plight of the Jewish people.[26]

To understand the secular character of Zionism and to overemphasize its undeniable religious dimensions is to lay

25. Ibid., p. 247.

26. See Vital, *Origins of Zionism*, p. 375. Vital's excellent treatment concludes with the claim that what kept Zionists together and their institutions intact was that the terrible "social reality was always stronger than the disputes about it." The misery of the Jews' condition in the Pale of Settlement, Galicia, and Rumania could not wait for relief: it outweighed "both the force of inertia and of religious teaching." To this was added anti-Semitism in the West.

One can agree with Vital's emphasis, but when he sets the force of "religious teaching" against the need for relief, one hesitates to concur. His conclusion at this point ignores his own opening chapter, which points to the pervasive religious substructure of all Jewish thinking about The Land. The misery of Jews would not in itself have been creatively dynamic had it not been sustained by hope, however variously expressed. Misery alone breeds despair. Did not the endemic hope for The Land, even when denied its religious character, provide the light at the end of the tunnel oneself open to the temptation of giving to the doctrine of The Land a significance which in much of Judaism would be a distortion.[27]

---

which helped to sustain Jews? The history of movements of social reform, and of revolutions, sufficiently indicates that total misery in itself merely leads to inertia. Such movements have usually been born out of an element other than misery itself.

27. The position indicated in our treatment of Zionism is reinforced in a private communication from Mr. Abba Eban, which he has allowed us to publish. A question that has frequently puzzled me is why the founders of the state of Israel agreed to the creation of a state in which the areas significant in Jewish religious tradition were not included, that is, Judah and Samaria, the West Bank, and the totality of Jerusalem itself. I posed this question to Mr. Abba Eban, who responded as follows:

The founders of political Zionism regarded the Bible as a general source of legitimacy for reestablishing a Jewish state. At no time, however, did any of them, including the religious parties, consider themselves to be committed to the ancient distributions of Jewish population within Eretz Israel. The League of Nations' mandate recognised the right of the Jewish people to reconstitute its national home "*in* Palestine." A Zionist text calling for the "reconstitution of Palestine as the national home of the Jewish people" was rejected by the international community. Thus, there is a partitionist implication inherent in the development of Jewish statehood from the very moment when that statehood became a concrete political prospect.

The settlement policy of the Zionist movement was based on the aim of avoiding any conflict with existing demographic realities. The idea was to settle Jews where Arabs were *not* already in firm possession. Thus, instead of settling in Jaffa with the aim of outnumbering the Arabs, the early Zionists established their own separate city of Tel Aviv. In agricultural settlement, they looked for areas which were empty of Arabs. Since the main concentrations of Arab population were in areas associated with the ancient Jewish kingdoms, it followed that modern Jewish settlement was destined to concentrate itself elsewhere, namely the land of the Philistines in the coastal plain, as well as in the valleys of Jezreel and Esdraelon, which Arab populations had avoided because of insalubrious conditions. In other words, the principle for Jewish settlement and land purchase was always empirical and contemporary, never religious or historical.

In the United Nations' discussions leading to Israel's membership of the UN, we relied on the general premise of a historic connection, but made no claim whatever for the inclusion of particular areas on our side of the Partition boundary on the grounds of ancient connection. Since Hebron was full of Arabs, we did not ask for it. Since Beersheba was virtually empty, we put in a successful claim. The central Zionist thesis was that there existed suffcient room within Eretz Israel for densely populated Jewish society to be established without displacing Arab populations, and even without intruding upon their deep-rooted social cohesion.

In *The Idea of the Jewish State*, Ben Halpern presents a rather more complicated picture (see, especially, pp. 41, 47). I have unfortunately not, as yet, been able to locate the works of A. Ruppin, to which Mr. Eban refers.

3
The Contradiction Resolved

So far we have pinpointed what appears to be a contradiction: much of the theology and history of Judaism in its main expressions points to The Land as of its essence: the history of Judaism, however, seems also to offer serious qualifications of this. Can this contradiction be resolved? We suggest that the Jews' understanding of their own history comes to terms precisely with this contradiction and resolves it in life, *solvitur ambulando*.

We have appealed to history in support of the claim that exile as much as, if not more than, life in The Land has significantly marked Jewish history. The force of that appeal must in no way be belittled. Taken in isolation, however, it is misleading, because in the Jewish experience, both religious and secular, exile has always coexisted with the hope of a return to The Land. It might well be argued that the Jewish people would probably have gradually disintegrated and ceased to be without that hope. Here the distinction between exile (*galûth*) and simple dispersion is important: the two terms are easily confused.[1] Statistics

1. The incidence of these terms is significant. It is interesting to note that *diaspora* never translates the Hebrew words *gôlâh* or *galûth*, which denote the process of deportation and the state of those deported. These terms are rendered in LXX by *aichmalôsia* (captivity); *apoikesia* (emigration); *metoikesia* (deportation); and *paroikia* (sojourning). These pejorative terms were abandoned in turn in favor of *diaspora*. The reason for this, according to F. Rendtorff and K. L. Schmidt, was a desire to give expression to the benefits as well as the disadvantages of the Diaspora for the

cannot be supplied, but many Jews throughout the centuries have voluntarily chosen to live outside The Land, and many still do. The dispersion of such is not exile. But, in most periods, most Jews have had no choice, and ultimately owe their place in the various countries of the world to the enforced exile of their ancestors. It is with these "exiles"—not simply the "dispersed"—that we are here concerned. That Jews outside Palestine conceived of their existence not simply as a dispersion meant that, wherever they were, they were still bound symbolically, theologically as well as historically, to their home base, to Eretz Israel: they were not simply scattered. The Diaspora maintained the notion of its existence as a *galûth*, exile.

The Jews have been sustained, as a people, largely by the way in which they have traditionally interpreted their own

Jewish people. (See K. L. Schmidt, "Diaspora.") The terms *galûth* and *diaspora* demand further research. A beginning is made on *galûth* in R. E. Price, "A Lexiographical Study of *glh, šbh* and *šwb* in Reference to Exile in the Tanach."

For various approaches to history among Jews, see Lionel Kochan, *The Jew and His History* (reviewed by U. Tal in *Journal of Jewish Studies* 31 [Autumn 1980]: 252–57). For attitudes to The Land and The State in present-day Israel, see a clear summary statement by Michael Shashar, "The State of Israel and the Land of Israel," *The Jerusalem Quarterly* (Fall 1980); and also by Yeshayahu Leibowitz, "State and Religion," *ibid.* (Winter 1980). Particularly noteworthy is "The Land and the State of Israel in Israeli Religious Life," by U. Tal in *Proceedings of the Rabbinical Assembly*, 76th Annual Convention, (Grossinger, N.Y.: Rabbinical Assembly, 1977) 38: 1–40. See also Tal's paper "Historical and Metahistorical Self-Views" in *Religious Zionism*, forthcoming at the University of Tel Aviv Press, 1981; and also an interview with Tal on "The Nationalism of Gush Emunim in Historical Perspective" in *Forum on the Jewish People, Zionism and Israel*, no. 36 (Fall/Winter 1979), published by the World Zionist Organization, Jerusalem.

history as revealing a recurring pattern of exile and return to Eretz Israel. In the various countries of their abode, they have understood their existence as essentially transient or pilgrim, always en route to The Land. The Scriptures point to the patriarchs in search of The Land; the settlement of The Land is followed by the descent—in this case an economically necessary "exile"—into Egypt, followed by a return thence and resettlement in The Land. Later there is another exile to Babylon, this time enforced, and again a return in the time of Cyrus. The Hellenistic period saw the rise of a vast dispersion, both voluntary and forced, and the first-century revolt against Rome was followed by an exile which continued right down to this century, again leading to a return. Jews have constantly been conditioned by the harsh actualities of their history to think of return. Even the so-called "nonexilic" exile of Jews in Moorish and Christian Spain, where Jews for long enjoyed virtual integration into the societies in which they lived, ended in disaster and a fresh dispersion. The pattern of exile and return has been historically inescapable, and has underlined the belief that there is an unseverable connection between Yahweh, His people and His Land. History has reinforced theology to deepen the consciousness of Jews that The Land was always "there"—whether to be wrestled with in occupation or to return to from exile. As Professor Edmund Jacob has written in a brilliant lecture: "En effet, toute l'histoire d'Israël peut être envisagée comme une lutte pour la terre et avec la terre, comme le combat de Jacob était une lutte avec Dieu et pour Dieu."[2]

The implication of the acceptance of exile in the Tanak and by the rabbis is, moreover, that the relation between Israel and The Land is not simply to be understood in terms

2. E. Jacob, *Israël dans la perspective biblique*, p. 22.

of occupation or possession of it, and that the destruction of The Land should not, and does not, spell the destruction of the people. Israel has no perpetual, inalienable right to The Land; it can lose possession of it. The Land, in turn, is not an end in itself, but a means whereby the people of Israel are the better to fulfill their destiny—that is, to fulfill the demands of the Torah. Possession of The Land depended on fulfillment of the commandments (Deut. 11:14). Israel's relation to The Land was highly dialectical, holding in tension the need to possess The Land and the recognition that it could always by its infidelity be exiled from it—though exiled only to return.

In Jewish tradition, return could be conceived of in two ways. Nonreligious Jews in every age could interpret it as a political event—that is, as simply the restoration to Jews of political rights in their own land denied them after the collapse of the Jewish revolts in 70 and 132–35 C.E. (unrealistic as it must have often seemed to non-Jews). Such Jews have often understood exile and return in secular political-economic terms. In principle, so did many of the sages. The rabbinical leaders never recognized that the conquest of Eretz Israel by a foreign power could be legitimized: the Romans were usurpers, their agents thieves. The Land belonged to Israel because Yahweh had promised it to her. So in the Mishnah it is implicitly regarded as legitimate to evade Roman taxes (Mishnah Nedarim 3:4). The ruling powers were to be given obedience, but not cooperation—even in the interest of law and order. To the rabbis, the return would involve control of The Land.

But, again to the frequent astonishment of non-Jews, much more was involved than this to the sages and their followers, who perceived the dimensions of the question as primarily spiritual. To them, just as exile was conceived of as the outcome of the wrath of God, so too the return was to be the manifestation of His gracious purpose for them despite their past disobedience. From this point of view, the return was to be a redemption. What to non-Jews was primarily, if not always exclusively, of political significance, for religious Jews was of theological significance.

But this neat division between religious and non-religious Jews, like all such divisions, is misleading. Neither category was watertight; they interacted and were mutually stimulating, as well as being highly variegated. The concepts of the one permeated those of the other to make for infinite complexity. Although the secular thought in terms of return, and the religious in terms of redemption, ultimately, because of the nature of the Tanak, upon which, whether consciously or unconsciously, they both drew, the two points of view often dissolved into each other. In the Zionist movement, secular, socialistic Jews constantly found themselves "at home" with the religious elements in the movement, who did not share their political views but provided a common ambit of thought on, or sentiment for, The Land.

Nevertheless, just as with seeing the return in terms of the restoration of political rights, seeing it in terms of redemption has certain consequences. If the return were an act of divine intervention, it could not be engineered or forced by political or any other human means: to do so would be impious. That coming was best served by waiting in obedience for it: men of violence would not avail to bring it in. The rabbinic aloofness to messianic claimants sprang not only from the history of disillusionment with such, but from this underlying, deeply engrained attitude.

It can be claimed that under the main rabbinic tradition Judaism condemned itself to powerlessness. But recognition of powerlessness (rather than a frustrating, futile, and tragic resistance) was effective in preserving Judaism in a very hostile Christendom, and therefore had its own brand of "power." True to the paradoxical realism of Judaism, moreover, "orthodoxy" did not allow the belief that the return depended upon Divine initiative to prevent it from always holding in principle that a fully dedicated obedience to the Torah could bring about that initiative. In the Lurianic Qabbalah, for example, this connection was particularly active.

For the purpose of this essay, the significance of the attitude towards their existence in foreign lands and towards the hope of return which we have ascribed to religous Jews is that despite their apparent quietism in the acceptance of the Torah as a portable land—and this, it must be emphasized, is only in an interim ethic—the hope for a return to Eretz Israel was never far from their consciousness. They remained true "in spirit" to the territorial theology of the Tanak and of the other sources of their faith. Except perhaps in modern Germany, where they often thought themselves to be "at home," religious Jews generally, especially those of the most traditionalist persuasion, have regarded any existing, present condition outside The Land as temporary. If not always pilgrims to it in a literal sense, they have always set their faces towards The Land. This fidelity has, in turn, strengthened the continuing belief in the "umbilical", eternal connection between the people and its Land and helped to preserve for that Land its "sacredness."In the experience of Jews, theology has informed the interpretation of history, and history in turn has confirmed the theology.

In reflecting on the answer finally to be given to the question presented to us in the light of the evidence so inadequately set forth here, an analogy from Christian ecclesiology suggests itself. In Roman Catholicism and High Church Anglicanism, the distinction has often been drawn, in discussions of the apostolic episcopate, between what is of the *esse* and what of he *bene esse* of the Christian Church. That episcopate is claimed by some to be constitutive of the Church—that is, to be of its essence, so that where there is no "apostolically" ordained bishop, there can be no true Church. To others, it is simply a means of securing the well-being of the Church. Is this distinction applicable to the way in which the mainstream of Judaism has conceived of The Land? Judaism has certainly been compelled by the actualities of history to accept exile as a permanent and major mark of its existence and as a source of incalculable benefit. Has it, then, by implication, recognized—despite the witness of most of its classical sources and, indeed, it might be argued, in conformity with much in them—that while life in The Land is of the *bene esse* of all Jewish religious existence, it is not of the *esse*? Moses desired to be in The Land so that he might have the possibility of achieving greater obedience to the Torah: that he did not enter it was a very great deprivation. But it was not fatal to his existence as a Jew (*BT* Sotah 14a). The greatest blessing is to live in The Land, but this is not absolutely essential. A Jew can remain true to his Judaism, however inadequately by the standards set by the sources, as long as he is loyal to the Torah. He can continue in his faith outside The Land, but not outside the Torah: not The Land, but the Torah is the essence of Judaism; it is its very relation to the Torah that endows the Land with holiness. It is highly significant that the capture of Jerusalem by King David is not commemorated in any special festival. Comparably, the feast of Hannukah commemorates the victory of the Maccabees not because they captured Jerusalem but because they were victorious in a war in defence of the Torah. No less significant is the fact that the Torah is not called the Torah of Israel, but the Torah of the Name (i.e., God). Neither is The Land called The Land of Israel—which is the people of God and of the Torah. From this point of view, The Land is of the *bene esse*, not of the *esse* of the Jewish faith: to give any absolute or final significance to The Land would be a denial of Judaism. There is no little danger in using such terms as *terre mystique de l'Absolu* if the term "Absolute" is transferred to The Land itself.

Yet one is uneasy about the analogy, and that not only because the Torah itself and the Mishnah are so over-whelmingly concerned with The Land. The antithesis between *esse* and *bene esse*, conceptually valid as it may seem to be, does not do justice to the place of The Land. We suggest that the way in which the question of The Land was originally posed—that is, in terms of the essence of Judaism—may itself, in fact, be misleading and result in a misplacement in our answer. The term *essence* suggests the impersonal, and is as inadequate in dealing with The Land in Judaism as it is in dealing with Christianity, as for example it was used by Feuerbach and Harnack in the notion of the "essence of Christianity." Neher[3] and Lacocque[4] have pointed to the personification of The Land in Judaism in feminine terms. They perhaps go too far in ascribing to simile and figurative language an actual personalism. But it is well to recognize that The Land was called *Beulah* (the betrothed), and exaggerated as their claims may be, they do guard us against impersonalism in understanding the role of The Land. As F. W. Dillistone would put it, "The Land" is not space but a place.[5] It evokes immense and deep

3. A. Neher, *L'Existence Juive*.
4. A. Lacocque, "Une Terre qui découle de lait et de miel."
5. F. W. Dillistone, *Traditional Symbols and the Contemporary World*, chapter 6.

emotion among religious Jews. It presents a kind of personal challenge and offers a personal anchorage. The sentiment (a term here used in its strict psychological sense) for The Land" is so endemic among religious Jews (we are not here directly concerned with others) and so constantly reinforced by their sacred sources, liturgies, and observances that to set life in The Land against life outside The Land as *esse* against *bene esse* is to miss the point. It is better to put the question in another way and ask: does The Land lie at the heart of Judaism? Put in this more personal manner the question answers itself.

The intensely "personal" nature of the relationship between the people and The Land becomes clearest in the use of feminine marital terms to describe it. Martin Buber[6] did not hesitate to speak of the sacred marriage between The Land and the people of Israel, and that The Land is the spouse of Yahweh appears in many passages of the Tanak (Hos. 2:5–23; Jer. 3:19–20; Isa. 62:4; and the Song of Songs have been so understood).[7] This is related to the Baal worship of Canaan, but it recalls to us also the question of the existence of a Hebraic mother-goddess or goddesses. The issue is pointedly raised by Richard Rubenstein when he urges that "the rediscovery of Israel's earth and the lost divinities of that earth" enables the Jews of today to "come into contact with those powers of life and death which engendered man's feelings about Baal, Astarte, and Anath.

6. Martin Buber, *Israel und Palestina,* p. 11. It is significant that the word *'eretz* can be both masculine and feminine. The plural form is feminine, *'arâtzōth.*

7. These passages are not unambiguous. In taking them to refer not only to the people of Israel as married to Yahweh but also to The Land as so married, I follow Jacob, *Israël dans la perspective biblique.*

These powers have again become decisive in our religious life".[8] Along with The Land's rôle in the promise, and as the centre of the earth, Edmund Jacob has rightly identified the conjugal myth of the marriage of the people with The Land as the governing source for the doctrine of The Land in Judaism.[9] The mythological expressions which, in liturgy and in song, express the significance of The Land as such are unmistakably personal and powerful. Into the discussion of this question, reopened by Rubenstein, we are not competent to enter. We merely recognize that the doctrine of The Land has age-old mythological roots, not to be limited to the soil of Israel.

Just as Christians recognize "the scandal of particularity" in the Incarnation, in Christ, so for many religious Jews (though their particular doctrine is not so central as is the incarnation of Christ for Christians) there is a scandal of territorial particularity in Judaism. The Land is so embedded in the heart of Judaism, the Torah, that—so its sources, worship, theology, and often its history attest—it is finally inseparable from it. As J. Juster insisted, "Il faut . . . ne pas essayer de diviser des choses indivisibles."[10] However, all this being recognized, it remains to emphasize one thing. If by a territorial religion is meant, as is usually the case, "a cult whose constituency is a territorial group identified by common occupation of a particular

8. Rubenstein, *After Auschwitz*, p. 106. See, also, J. Z. Smith, *Map Is Not Territory*, p. 106, on the subject. Not all agree that the rediscovery to which Rubenstein refers is to be welcomed. Some look upon it as a retrogression to the territorial gods of ancient paganism (see J. J. Petuchowski, *Zion Reconsidered*, pp. 84–85).

9. E. Jacob, "Les Trois Racines d'une théologie de la 'Terre' dans l 'A.T."

10. Quoted in G. F. Moore, *Judaism*, I, 234.

land area, so that membership of the cult is in the final instance a consequence of residence and not kinship or ethnic designation,"[11] then Judaism is not a territorial religion: The Land is *not* of the essence.

11. J. M. Schoffeleers, *Guardians of the Land: Essays on the Central African Territorial Cults,* p. 1.

Epilogue: Reflexions on the Doctrine of The Land

What are we, finally, to make of this doctrine of The Land which gives theological significance—as it has been crudely put—"to a piece of real estate"? Many Jews, no less than Gentiles, have dismissed it as a bizarre and anachronistic superstition, unworthy of serious consideration. To many rationalists, and even humanists, especially since the En-lightenment,[1] in a rational universe the doctrine is an af-front. This response is generally coupled with the assump-tion that the doctrine is simply an aspect of that other doctrine of "chosenness" or "election" that—so it is claimed—has irrationally and arrogantly afflicted (a verb chosen advisedly) the Jewish people, the particularism of The Land being, in fact, an especially primitive expression of the unacceptable particularism of the Jewish faith.

Even when sponsored by such as Martin Buber, how-ever, the claim that the doctrine of The Land is altogether unique is now recognized to be hard to substantiate.[2] Mu-tatis mutandis, historians of religion, especially, have dis-

---

1. See Arthur Hertzberg, *The French Enlightenment and the Jews*, passim.

2. In the view of J. Weston Le Bar, Distinguished Professor of Anthropology, Duke University, Judaism is unique in its insis-tence on The Land as "chosen" and "promised" (oral commu-nication). But the notion of "manifest destiny" in American his-tory, for example offers at least a parallel.

covered similar, if not identical, attitudes towards their particular lands among other peoples. The Jews' interpretation of The Land as an enclave in the wilderness, and as the pillar and centre of the cosmos, and their experience of separation from The Land as an exile of devastating chaos, find parallels in other traditions. However much a mark of "primitive" Jewish particularism, the doctrine has its roots in what seems to be a universal human need.[3]

It is not surprising, therefore, that recently the deep concern with The Land in Judaism has been approached afresh. Some interpret it psychologically: the doctrine is simply the communal or societary expression of the psychological need of every child or person to be "rooted" in his or her own home or space, to cling to accustomed ground. Others have emphasized its biological roots. Robert Ardrey has urged that, in insisting on their eternal relationship with The Land, the Jews are simply obeying what he calls "a territorial imperative," which governs human no less than animal behavior.[4] "Territory" is in essence a psychological expression, and the possession of a territory serves the purposes of security, stimulation, and identity.

We have elsewhere subjected Ardrey's position to criticism.[5] Certain of his historical data are questionable, and he fails to do justice to the specifically religious dimensions of Israel's relation to The Land of Yahweh. That relation was not simply "territorial," in Ardrey's sense, but also theological. So, too, the role of the Law cannot be ex-

3. Professor D. Daube, in a private communication, urges this. In his judgment this psychological fact gives a profound meaning and universal ground for the attachment to The Land.

4. See GL, appendix 3, pp. 405–8, on Ardrey's *The Territorial Imperative*.

5. Ibid. For a severe critique of Ardrey, see also Ashley Montague, "The New Litany of Innate Depravity, or Original Sin Revisited."

plained solely in terms of the hostility to outside pressures to which Ardrey refers. The commandments were not so much a fence around the Jews, as he insists, as they were around the Torah itself. I also understand that many scientists qualified to examine his concept of the territorial imperative find it untenable.

But Ardrey's insistence on the importance of territory and its loss for a people can hardly be gainsaid. Aspects of Jewish history confirm him in this. Apart from psychological consequences of deterritorialization too obvious to need discussion, there are deep cultural deprivations. The character of Yiddish illustrates how "unnatural," in the strict sense, are the results of the radical divorce from The Land in the literature of the deterritorialized. That language was the product of generations of Jews who lived in ghettoes in various countries in Europe, but understood their homeland to be elsewhere. In general, for example, the ghetto Jew knew the flora and fauna of Palestine better than he did those of Poland or Russia. In *The World of Scholem Aleichem*, Maurice Samuel writes:

Yiddish is a folk language, but unlike all other folk languages, it has no base in nature. It is poor, almost bankrupt, by comparison with other languages in the vocabulary of field and forest and stream. . . . Yiddish has almost no flowers . . . the very words for the common flowers which are familiar to city dwellers everywhere are lacking in Yiddish. Yiddish is a world almost devoid of trees. . . . The animal world is almost depopulated in Yiddish . . . the skies are practically empty of birds. . . . There is likewise a dearth of fish . . . there are no nature descriptions to be found anywhere in Yiddish prose or poetry. . . . All these expressions and perceptions were lacking because their material was withheld from the Jews. There were large areas of what we generally call folk self-expression to which the Jews were forever strangers.[6]

6. M. Samuel, *The World of Scholem Aleichem*, pp. 194–96.

This needs no comment. Language is the life-blood of a culture. It is not surprising that many Jews have seen in the amazing renaissance of Hebrew in modern Israel a sure sign of the messianic character of that state.

Then again, there are the political deprivations incurred in deterritorialization. Hannah Arendt rightly emphasized the degeneration suffered by Jews denied political self-expression and control of their own land—in her view the most tragic of all denials.[7] The American Indians leap to mind. And one has simply to ask, by way of a parallel example, what "the Southland" (a significant term: one does not speak of "the Northland" although one does speak of the North and the South) would have developed into had not Southerners been allowed to reenter the mainstream of the political life of the United States, to appreciate something of the degree of the deprivation that deterritorialized Jews have suffered over the centuries, and the overwhelming intensity with which the emergence of the Jewish state was acclaimed. From one angle age-long adherence to the doctrine of The Land can be understood as a protest against deterritorialization. In varying degrees, however, we are all now children of the Enlightenment, a movement which searched for universals in every sphere,[8] and recognized no particularism or uniqueness, least of all of a geographic-religious kind. The Enlightenment still predisposes us to pass by, and often to scorn, the notion of a particular Land for Judaism. The very words "Chosen People," "Chosen Land" strike an unsympathetic chord. Christian and even Jewish thinkers (under the influence of the former) have preferred to deal with Judaism in conceptual categories derived from

7. See Hannah Arendt, *The Jew as Pariah*.

8. See Herzberg, *Enlightenment and the Jews*; also J. A. Sanders, "Text and Canon," pp. 27–28.

Christian theology instead of in terms of the geographic and other data provided by the earlier faith itself, and have in particular concentrated on time to the neglect of space.[9] For example, it is only very recently that attempts have been made to ask how the writers of the New Testament, the foundation document of Christianity, reacted to the doctrine of The Land. The reasons for this tardiness are not only that the earliest Jewish Christians have left so few documents, and that the early Christian movement quickly became predominantly Gentile, so that the New Testament is largely concerned with non-Jews, to whom the question of The Land was not primary. Beginning with the New Testament, and certainly since St. Augustine, Christianity

9. See *GL*, p. 66, n. 4; also, typically, Martin Buber, ed., *Jüdische Künstler*, p. 7: "The Jew of antiquity was more an audient than a visual being and felt more in terms of time than of space," Buber writes. André Neher is more balanced: "Mais Israël en découvrant le temps a aussi découvert l 'espace qui est cet espace réduit de la terre d'Israël, couronné par Jerusalem"(*Rencontre*, p. 78). This book has concentrated on territory and bypassed the question of time. My insistence on the recurring pattern of exile and return in Jewish history may be taken as being more in accord with a cyclical view of time (usually associated with the Greeks) than with the dominant view of time in the Bible, which has often been taken as linear (see, especially, O. Cullman, *Christ and Time*). But the recurring "fulfillment" pattern coexists with a search for the transcendent, and there *is* a denouement to the recurring pattern in rabbinic Judaism and Christianity—in the former in the map without territory, the portable Torah, and in the latter in the advent of Christ, although both religions also retain hope for the ultimate future. (In much of Zionism, the denouement comes to be regarded as politically achieved in the emergence and creation of the state of Israel.) See, further, *GL*, p. 36, where I quote G. von Rad, *The Problem of the Hexateuch*, p. 297: "Promises which have been fulfilled in history are not thereby exhausted of their content but remain as promises on a different level."

in its major expressions has substituted for the holiness of place—The Land, Jerusalem, the Temple—the holiness of Christ. The Land—although called Holy in Christianity—is ultimately incidental in Christian affection and faith. Life "in Christ" replaces life "in The Land" as the highest blessing, so that the traditional Jewish doctrine of the unseverability of Land, people, and God is not upheld.[10]

But all this has been at a price. In understandably insisting that the territorial doctrine has been transcended in the Gospel, Chrisitanity has often failed to do justice to the

10. No effort is made here to deal with the specifically Christian responses to the territorial doctrine of Judaism. The evidence for these in the New Testament was examined in *GL*, pp. 161–376. The achievement of a largely unexpressed consensus among the main bodies of Christians was long in emerging (see, for example, R. J. Vair, "The Old Testament Promise of the Land as Reinterpreted in First- and Second-Century Christianity"). Mutatis mutandis, there has continued to be a degree of literal adherence to the territorial dimension of Judaism, especially among certain fundamentalist sects and the Mormons (see W. D. Davies, "Israel, Mormons, and The Land," pp. 80–92). In its dominant expressions, however, Christianity has demanded the deterritorialization of the theological tradition it inherited from the people of Israel. But such deterritorialization does not conflict with the positive aspects of the doctrine of The Land expressed here. In "Judaïsme et Christianisme," a response to Professor David Flusser's review of *GL*, for example, Father Pierre Benoit observed:

> [Le Professeur Flusser] reproche aux Chrétiens de réclamer des Juifs qu'ils cessent d'être des Juifs, et deviennent des Gentils dans le Christ. Je réponds à ce grief par une distinction. Le dilemme énoncé par Flusser est ambigu: il parle du Juif devenant chrétien "sans abolir le caractère et le mode qui lui sont propres, et sans renoncer aux promesses spéciales qu'il a reçues de Dieu," ou au contraire "en abandonnant le caractère spécial et les prétentions spéciales du Juif." L'alternative est mal proposée dans le mesure où elle ne distingue pas entre l'aspect ethnico-politique que est en effet propre au peuple particulier

cultural and historical dimension which that doctrine preserved. Judaism's insistence that the people of Israel needed
a land through which and within which fully to express its
identify, that that people had to have a "space" which it

---

d'Israël, et l'aspect proprement religieux que devait selon le
plan de Dieu s'étendre en s'élargissant à toute la communauté
humaine." [p. 149]
The Christian demand for the deterritorialization of faith does not
of necessity ignore or deny the natural and justifiable ethnic-
political necessities of the Jewish people. The claims of Jewish
ethnicity were wrestled with in the earliest period of the Christian
movement (see W. D. Davies, "Paul and the People of Israel,"
especially pp. 31–36). That they were subsequently ignored is part
of the tragedy of Christian history. For the sake of completeness,
albeit not to exonerate Christianity for its neglect of the problem
of ethnicity and territory in Judiasm, it should be noted that some
expressions of Judaism itself have been equally concerned to detach themselves from that problem. Thus B. M. Bokser, in a
review of *GL*, can write of the rabbis after 70 C.E.:
    Torah, as the rabbis saw it, contains the key to the world and
    to the nature of existence. Of course, some rabbinic circles
    provided means to remember the Temple. But holiness was
    now divorced from a single place. The way of Torah enabled
    each individual to bring holiness into daily life, no longer by
    means of the Temple. The new set of metaphors reflects a
    conscious discontinuity, in contrast to the Christian concept
    which merely continued the old motif of holiness of Temple in
    a new way. The holiness of a single person, Jesus, replaces that
    of a single place, in faith, the Christian community represents
    the true Temple. *In contrast, Torah, in the emerging rabbinic move-
    ment, was not just a comfort to Jews without a Temple, but was the
    basis for a new piety, one quite different from that of Christianity and
    the Second Temple.* [p. 74. Italics added.]
That deterritorialization was only slowly achieved in Christianity
appears from Vair, "The Old Testament Promise of the Land";
see, too, Max Warren, "The Concept and Historic Experience
with Land in Major Western Religious Traditions," in the *Proceedings of the Jerusalem Colloquium on Religion, Peoplehood, Nation,
and Land*, and the discussion in ibid., pp. 201–8.

could turn into its own "place," probably points to a truth about all people, ultimately even for nomadic people, who, where opportunity offers, tend to seek a place in which to settle. Usually between nomadic and settled peoples, where they are contiguous, there is constant movement from one to the other.[11] Nor should it be overlooked that nomads lay claim to the "territory" of their particular wanderings, even though they do not settle down in it. A human community needs a geographic dimension of its own within which and through which to express itself. Judaism's insistence that the occupancy of The Land is not absolute but conditioned by obedience to the Torah, that observance and nonobservance of the commandments have geographic, territorial, and cosmic consequences, points to the truth that ecology is indissoluble from morality, land and law being mutually dependent, and that a people is ultimately responsible for the maintenance of its "place."

The Jewish people's experience of exile as a "chaos" to be overcome, although often creative, reveals the price probably paid by all peoples whose territorial roots are cut.[12] The

11. See Lesley Hazleton, "The Forgotten Israelis."

12. On exile as "chaos," see J. Z. Smith, *Map Is Not Territory*, p. 119. The views of Sir Isaiah Berlin seem largely to converge with those expressed here (see J. Lieberson and S. Morgenbesser, "The Choices of Isaiah Berlin," a review of *The Idea of Freedom: Essays in Honor of Isaiah Berlin*, ed. Alan Ryan, and Berlin's *Against the Current: Essays on the History of Ideas*). Berlin agrees with Herder that eluding or denying the need to be rooted in a particular group robs men of dignity and self-identity. Different nations or cultures can emerge alongside one another, respecting each other's activities, without engendering conflict. "The values of a group are neither portable nor exchangeable but unique, historical, irreplaceable," write Lieberson and Morgenbesser (p. 11). So Herder, and so Berlin apparently. It is imperative to recognize that the self-expression of a group or people, and even

Jewish engagement with The Land is, therefore, a para-
digm of most, if not all peoples' engagement with their
lands. 'Abd Al-Tāfahum has expressed the same truth: "We
do not rightly understand the Old Testament's sense of
place and people unless we know that it mirrors and edu-
cates the self-awareness of all lands and dwellers. The na-
tionhood of Israel, the love of Zion, has its counterpart in
every continent."[13]

The struggles between Judaism and Christianity in past
centuries, when the latter in its mainstream chose disen-
landisement (to employ the ugly word used by 'Abd Al
Tāfahum), can no longer govern our thinking on the question of The Land. Without the concreteness of the demand
to express community in and through the actualities of
space—without the soiling of hands with the soil, so to
speak—we are in danger of unrealism. The false romanticism, the unrealism, and the individualistic, otherworldly
spirituality and false dualism of much in Christian history,
although it has other sources in Hellenism and in recent
years in a revolt against technological secularism, may not
be wholly unconnected with the radical break with The

more of a nation, can be twisted into aggressive nationalism, as in
Europe and elsewhere in the nineteenth and twentieth centuries;
but its denial is as dangerous as its jingoistic affirmation. Such
doctrines as that of The Land are clearly and notoriously prone to
political and ideological distortion, especially when dressed up in
terms of psychology and biology. As Mr. Richard Holway has
reminded me, science tends to lend authority to any ideology.
Davidic imperial ambitions possibly influenced the doctrine of
The Land. But the misuse of a doctrine is no proof either of its
truth or falsity; its value can be assessed apart from its misuse. The
aim here has been to stimulate reflection on the meaning and value
of the doctrine of The Land, not to foreclose discussion of its
beneficial potentialities or dangers.

13. 'Abd Al-Tāfahum, "Doctrine."

Land as much of Judaism has understood it. It has been held
by some that this was one of the factors that ultimately led
to the massive protest of early Marxism against false spirituality. The events of our time, in which we have seen the
horrendous consequences of deterritorializing peoples in
the Far East, the Near East, and Europe, have confirmed
that this is to cut their deepest psychological and cultural
roots. Many Christian peoples in the West have often been
able to ignore these consequences and to escape conceptually into an unrooted universalism. But this is because
they have for the most part been able to assume their rootedness and have never known any territorial break comparable with that experienced by Jews, nor been compelled
to come to terms even with the possibility of such. The
uniqueness of the Jewish doctrine lies not in the emotional
experience that gave it birth, however, but in the theological intensity with which it is held. At this point, the choice
is clear. One may assume, in the manner of modern ratio-
nalism, that Jewish religion, as is the case with all religions,
is the natural outgrowth of a people's efforts to ensure its
own survival and find answers to the problems of existence. If so, the theological aspect of the doctrine of The
Land can be dismissed.[14] Or one may follow the path suggested by Amos Wilder:

14. The issue has again been renewed in a very important study
by Norman K. Gottwald, *The Tribes of Yahweh*. Even had this
come to hand earlier, I do not have the competence to assess
adequately its massive knowledge and honest wrestling with
themes related to that dealt with here. If I understand Gottwald
aright, he regards the doctrine of chosenness to be an outgrowth
of the sociological context of the early tribes of Israel. These tribes
differed radically from their neighbors in various significant ways
and strove to preserve or ensure this difference through the development of that doctrine (see pp. 692–93, 702 f., 799, n. 639). This
means, it seems to me, that the theology of the doctrine is dis-

solved into, or absorbed by, sociology. At the risk of impertinence in responding to such an erudite volume in a footnote, I hesitatingly submit two reflections.

First, the doctrine of Israel as the "Chosen People," with which is tied up the doctrine of The Land, certainly only reached definiteness in the postexilic period, however much it may be related to the earlier sociological context described by Gottwald. The theological terms *baḥar* (to choose) and *bâḥûr* (chosen), used in connection with the people of Israel, are creations of the Deuteronomic school and of Deutero-Isaiah respectively—that is, they emerged at a time much later than that dealt with by Gottwald (see T. C. Vriezen, *Die Erwählung Israels nach dem A. T.*, and H. H. Rowley, *The Biblical Doctrine of Election*).

And, secondly, I may put the same kind of simple question to Gottwald that I posed to H. R. Trevor-Roper, who found the clue to the peculiarity of Israel's history in its geographical context (see *GL*, p. 89, n. 27). Until Gottwald's analysis is further examined, can we be sure that the sociological context of the tribes of Israel was unique? We may presume that they shared much of their geographical and, however distinctive, surely also much of their sociological background with other contemporary and contiguous groups. Why, then, should the doctrine of chosenness and of The Land emerge only among them? Gottwald acutely and impressively raises again an old question: does the recognition of the uniqueness of the sociological context of the early tribes of Israel (if such uniqueness be admitted) adequately account for the distinctiveness of their theology? Can we finally dissolve theology into sociology in the study of Jewish history? It is undeniable that the sociological *conditions* the theological. But does it *determine* the latter? Was it not precisely the peculiarity of its religious experience—that is, its experience of a revelation of the Divine— that explains the very radical difference between the response of the tribes of Israel to the surrounding milieu and that of other contemporary and contiguous groups? Backgrounds and influences, sociological, historical, and other, are important for the understanding of the doctrine of chosenness and of The Land, as of other doctrines. But Judaism as a phenomenon in human history must be seen in terms of depths as well as of horizontal links. Here the idea of revelation has its rights. In a letter to me in 1976 commenting on the mysterious faith which goes back to Abra-

There is an inseparable link between God's People, Law and Land. Without this "materialism" Judaism could not have made its fundamental contribution to Christianity, nor could it continue to bear its full witness to the world. It is true that the new faith universalized Zion. But the families and kindreds and peoples in Christendom have each their own form of rootedness and love of land; and God blesses the rules in and through these dimensions— but also limits and judges them all, including Zionism, in terms of his wider purposes. . . .

How far from understanding the human texture of God's working are all these mysticisms and spiritualisms which attract so many today![15]

Wilder's reference to the judgment on all nations leads us to the final stage of our response to the territorial doctrine of Judaism. By some strange alchemy this most earthly doctrine has often, apparently without difficulty, been transformed almost to its opposite. The Land has been spiritualized and transcendentalized—that is, it has been

---

ham, Dr. J. S. Whale put the matter forcibly [to make his words directly pertinent in response to Gottwald, "born of social circumstances" has been inserted after "ideology"]:

> What if so thoroughgoing and absolute a belief in God and his covenantal purpose, the *Sh'ma'* . . . should mean that here in Abraham ideology [born of social circumstances] really becomes theology? What if the obsessive, subjective "cognition" expressed in the *Sh'ma'* should point to objective reality? . . . What if the Hexateuch should be right and Marcion wrong?

To answer the question thus posed in the negative is to reduce Judaism and Christianity to a tragic illusion, however many ways that illusion may or may not be conceded to have been efficacious and beneficial. Ben Gurion could treat this illusion with levity, jauntily claiming that, "God did not create the Jews, the Jews created God." No one could accuse Gottwald of such levity. But does his position finally lead to any other conclusion than that of Ben Gurion?

15. In a private letter dated 3 October 1979.

made into a symbol of an ideal order either in this world or in the supernatural "world to come." Jews and Christians have both been engaged in this exercise across the centuries. The evidence for this in Judaism is clear in the Mishnah and earlier. In both Eastern and Western Christianity, such transcendentalizing and spiritualizing has persisted from the first century to the present—for example, in the hope for "a land of pure delight, where saints immortal reign" and for "Jerusalem the Golden." It is natural to see in all this simply a means of depriving the doctrine of The Land of the "crass" materiality which makes it a scandal to the "spiritual," and of circumventing the problem posed by territorial particularity both for Judaism and Christianity. But the process of transcendentalizing and spiritualizing The Land is more than this. It points to the recognition in both religions that, however desirable, the fulfillment of the terrestrial hope for The Land, or for any land, would not suffice to assuage the more than terrestrial aspirations of Israel or of any people. As Lurianism among many other movements shows, Israel and humanity as a whole have been concerned not only with a terrestrial destiny, but—so to put it—with what will be "when earth and man are gone / and suns and universes cease to be," when all terrestrial concerns have been swallowed up in "that day" when the whole temple of man's achievement will be buried in the debris of a universe in ruins. The hope for "The Land," transcendentalized and spiritualized, has enabled many to face "that day," and given assurance that their destiny lies in an eternal order, which "eye hath not seen nor ear heard." Paradoxically, The Land as actual geographic reality has sustained the people of Israel in its historical terrestrial pilgrimage. In the twentieth century this paradox is particularly significant. A new sensitivity, born of our experience in the space age, to our common perilous existence

on what Archibald MacLeish calls "the little, lonely, float-
ing planet, that tiny raft in the enormous empty night"
which we call earth, has made us more acutely conscious of
the questionableness of overemphasizing territorial divisions, however desirable. Simultaneously, on the contrary,
our awareness of spatial immensities has increased the felt
need to have "roots," "a place," "a territory." The need to
be rooted, which engendered among Jews the doctrine of
The Land anchored in the will of the Deity, is now more
than ever a living need for every people. And, at the same
time, the transitoriness and precariousness of human existence in the nuclear age compels a search for "The Land"
which defies time and space. The doctrine of The Land as
cherished by Judaism and reinterpreted both in that faith
and in Christianity, points to the twofold human need for
terrestrial roots and for the transcendent. The words of
Psalm 62:11 can be said of it: "One thing God has spoken:
two things have I learnt."

Finally, it must be recognized that, whether convincing
or not, any effort to discover meaning in Judaism's understanding of The Land will appear to two kinds of Jews as
irrelevant. The rabbis often sought what they called the
grounds or reasons for the commandments, which so often
appeared irrational, but only within limits. In the last re-
sort, they submitted to the impregnable, infallible rock of
the Tanak, which inseparably connected a chosen land with
a chosen people. "The essence of Judaism," it has been
asserted, "is the affirmation that the Jews are the chosen
people; all else is commentary."[16] In its overemphasis on
the isolation of one aspect of the Tanak, this is an exagger-

16. A. Hertzberg, *The Condition of Jewish Belief,* p. 90. Com-
pare D. Patterson, *The Foundations of Modern Hebrew Literature*
(London: Liberal Jewish Synagogue Press, 1961), pp. 7–8, and
"Modern Hebrew Literature Goes on Aliyah," *Journal of Jewish
Studies* 29 (Spring 1978): 75–84.

ation. But to religious Jews it is an exaggeration of a fundamental truth, carrying with it the eternal chosenness of The Land. To such Jews, rooted in their biblical certainties, such inquiry will appear irrelevant, trivial and, indeed, possibly impious.

But our efforts will seem equally irrelevant to Jews who have become detached, if not alienated, from the tradition of Judaism. The vast majority of Jews have been, and are, primarily concerned with survival and positive or negative assimilation in the lands where they find themselves,[17] and The Land is remote from the actualities of their lives. This was driven home very forcibly by Stanley Kunitz, who read parts of this work:

The critical question for me is the transition from historic Judaism to existential Jewishness, a phenomenon separable from religious practice. How to define it? I am reminded of the twelfth century poet, Yang Wan-li, one of the Four Masters of Southern Sung poetry, who, after experiencing "enlightenment," addressed his disciples in these terms.

Now what is poetry? If you say it is simply a matter of words, I will say, A good poet gets rid of words. If you say it is simply a matter of meaning, I will say, A good poet gets rid of meaning. But you will say, if words and meaning are gotten rid of, where is the poetry? To this I reply, Get rid of words and meaning, and there is still poetry.

So, too, one might say, "Get rid of Land and Torah, and you still have Jews." . . . The nostalgia of exile is entwined with the passion of survivorship, all of it steeped in vestigial tribal feelings. I have always assumed that states of crisis and paradox are part of the birthright.[18]

17. In this context, by negative assimilation is meant that process whereby Jews allow themselves to be swallowed up by a surrounding culture, so that they cease to be Jews; by positive assimilation, the effort made by Jews to make elements in surrounding cultures serve their own religious needs (see J. J. Petuchowski, *Zion Reconsidered*, pp. 124–29).

18. Letter to the author dated 28 February 1980.

The history of the doctrine of The Land is so complex that any endorsement of a simple literal understanding of the promise (as understood in Jewish orthodoxy) is critically unacceptable. At the same time the age-long engagement of Judaism with The Land in religious terms indicates that ethnicity and religion—despite the view expressed by Kunitz—are finally inseparable in Judaism. For us, nurtured though we be by the Enlightenment, that age long religious engagement constitutes part of the mystery of Israel in history. The obscurity of antiquity surrounds the origins of the doctrine of The Land with which we have been concerned. But although those origins and their detailed development ultimately elude us, what Jews believe to have happened has become a factor of undeniable historical and theological significance. That belief itself has become a historical datum. Its reality as an undeniable aspect of Judaism cannot be ignored. Across the centuries, Judaism has not usually displayed a rigid, unchangeable attitude towards and claim for The Land, but adaptability and compromise with the exigencies: its most characteristic aspect has been flexibility. A striking fact, previously mentioned, points to this: the term "holy land" seldom occurs in the Tanak, where the holiness of The Land is derivative (so that paradoxically the phrase "The Holy Land" is more native to Christians than to Jews). Later, the rabbis simply referred to The Land, even while revering it. Judaism has shied away from absolutizing the claims of The Land, subordinating them to the Torah.[19] It is arguable that the sober

19. See *GL*, p. 29. We have failed to indicate previously that the devotion to The Land in Judaism has been what might be called a "generalized" one. Apart from the unmistakable attachment to Jerusalem (which is the quintessence of The Land, see *GL*, pp. 131–50), Judaism has certainly not been marked by especial devotion to "holy places" to which historical events have

"myth" of Jamnia has longer and better served the survival of Jews and Judaism (if, indeed, these phenomena can ultimately be separated) than the more spectacular "myth" of Masada. In this century, no less than in the first, patient pliability and moderated enthusiasm are more likely to be constructive for Israel and the world than intransigence, however heroic.[20]

---

lent significance, as Christianity has been. This truism has often been expressed by claiming that Judaism reveres a "holy place"—The Land—and Christianity "holy places," such as Bethlehem, Galilee, Calvary and the site of the Resurrection. This explains why those Jews who settled in The Land did not concentrate on specific places (Jerusalem always being excepted), but were content to be "in The Land." In a letter dated 21 July 1980, Abba Eban writes:

> [We] distinguish between a *general* sentiment of attachment to the Land of Israel—and a selective or preferential approach to those specific parts of the land that are most associated with the biblical story. In Zionist ideology, the Land of Israel is a generic term, and the biblical literature is a strong factor in determining the legitimacy of the return. As I point out, however, in my letter, there is no evidence in Zionist practice or rhetoric of any lesser feeling [for] newly settled areas in comparison with those of which the names resound throughout history.

One interesting point to remember is that during the twenty years of Israeli statehood prior to 1967, there is hardly any nostalgic literature about Hebron, Shechem, Bethel, or other places that lay outside Israel's jurisdiction. Since 1967, Hebron is the only place where there has been an ambition to create a Jewish presence in direct association with biblical memories. Here too, however, the desire to renew the attachment owes just as much to the fact of a Jewish settlement up to 1929 as to Hebron's lineage in terms of biblical associations.

20. On the two "myths" of Masada and Jamnia (which are interpretations of actual events, although the rabbinic sources never refer to Masada), see an illuminating study by Baila R. Shargel, "The Evolution of the Masada Myth." There is evidence that the "Masadic myth" is being found wanting by twentieth-century Jewry, as it was by the sages in the first century.

Glossary

Apocalyptic: [from the Greek verb *apocaluptein*, "to reveal"] The doctrines about the end of all things (although the term also included other doctrines) and the extensive literature in which these doctrines are set forth. It flourished in the Hellenistic and Roman periods.

Apocrypha: The body of Jewish religious literature written between the second century B.C.E. and the second century C.E., not included in the Hebrew Bible, but incorporated in the Roman Catholic Old Testament. Other writings dealing with apocalyptic materials, generally referred to as the Pseudepigrapha, emerged in the same period. These Pseudepigrapha were thrust aside by the growth of rabbinical literature and were all but lost to the Jewish tradition, their preservation being largely due to the Christian Church. See *APOT* and a forthcoming collection edited by J. H. Charlesworth.

Diaspora: Literally, "dispersion." The Greek word used to refer to Jewish communities outside Palestine, both before and after the fall of Jerusalem in 70 C.E., composed both of voluntary and involuntary emigrants from Eretz Israel. There is much debate in modern Jewry as to whether the term still has overtones of "exile" (see n. 1 to chap. 3) or is simply to be taken as denoting the geographically widespread Jewish communities outside The Land.

Gemara: Literally, "completion," (i.e., of the Mishnah). The usual designation for the comment and discussion around the Mishnah. There are a Palestinian *gemara* and a Babylonian *gemara* to the Mishnah, but to many tractates no *gemara* is extant.

Haggadah: Literally, "narration." Generally the term denotes nonlegal elements in the Jewish sources and tradition— homilectics and morals, history and legend, scientific facts and philosophical reflections, biblical and rabbinical narratives. Specifically it describes the liturgical manual for the domestic service for Passover Eve.

Halakah: Literally, "the way to walk" (from the verb *hâlak*, "to walk"). The technical term for the whole body of rabbinic law and for particular provisions which by majority vote are accepted as legally binding. It covers trial, civil, ceremonial, and criminal law.

Hasidim: Literally, "pious ones." A group, usually taken to be the precursors of the Pharisees, which arose in the second century B.C.E., and at first participated in the Maccabaean revolt. The term is used to denote groups of pietists throughout the course of Jewish history and especially very pious Eastern European Jews of the eighteenth century, whose descendants can be found in colonies in the United States.

Jamnia: A city near Joppa where the rabbis gathered under the leadership of Johanan ben Zakkai after the Jewish Wars. According to modern scholars, the reorganization of post-70 C.E. Judaism and the collection and writing down of the halachic and haggadic oral traditions began there.

Lurianism: The school of mysticism founded by the Qabbalist Isaac Luria (1534–72) in Safed, Israel. It had a profound influence on the whole Jewish world, forming the basis for much of late hasidic thought.

Mekilta: One of the oldest of the Tannaitic Midrashim, giving an exposition of a large part of the book of Exodus, and dealing with almost all the laws of that book and with some of its most important narrative portions.

Midrash, pl. Midrashim: Literally, "investigation," "enquiry" (from the root *dârash*, "to inquire," "to investigate"). Midrash denotes writings that interpret Scripture in order to extract its full implications and meanings and also to impart contemporary relevance to biblical events. These writings are of two kinds: halakic midrashim, dealing with Mosaic Law, and haggadic midrashim, expounding nonlegal parts of Scripture. The Midrash Haggadah flourished greatly after the Mishnaic period.

Mishnah, The: [from the verb meaning "to repeat," "to learn," "to study," hence "learning," "study"] The systematized collection of laws (halakoth) finally codified by Judah the Prince around 220 C.E. More than simply a "code," the Mishnah is a textbook giving the essence of the Oral Law as it was known to the sages of that time, and remains the authoritative source for Jewish law. It consists of six orders (Shishah Sedarim), each divided into tractates, chapters, and paragraphs:

1. Zeraim ("Seeds"), eleven tractates, mainly on agricultural laws
2. Moed ("Appointed Times"), twelve tractates on the laws of festivals and feasts
3. Nashim ("Women"), seven tractates, chiefly on marriage, divorce, and vows
4. Nezikin ("Damages"), ten tractates on civil and criminal law
5. Kodashim ("Holy Things"), eleven tractates pertaining primarily to Temple services
6. Toharot ("Purity"), twelve tractates on the laws of ritual purity and impurity

The language of the Mishnah is in new (i.e., rabbinic) Hebrew as distinct from the classical language of the Bible.

Philo: Alexandrian Jewish philosopher (ca. 25 B.C.E.–40 C.E.) who combined contemporary Hellenistic philosophy and piety with belief in Revelation and Scripture.

Rashi: The name given to Solomon ben Isaac (1040–1105 C.E.), a leading commentator on the Bible and the Babylonian Talmud, who was born in Troyes, France. His widely acclaimed and influential commentary was published with the first edition of the Talmud, and except for modern editions of a few tractates, no edition of the *BT* has appeared without it.

Sabbatai Svi: Born in Smyrna in 1626, he claimed to be the Messiah, initiated an antinomian messianic movement which spread throughout Jewry with amazing rapidity. In 1666 he apostasized to Islam.

Talmud: Literally, "teaching," "study," "learning." The word is most commonly used as a comprehensive term for the Mishnah and Gemara taken together as a single unit. It is specifically applied to two compilations: the Palestinian Talmud, often wrongly referred to as the Jerusalem Talmud (Talmud Jerushalmi), and the Babylonian Talmud (Talmud Babli). These are the record of discussions over a period of about eight centuries by Jewish sages working continually in the academies of Palestine and Babylonia. To the sages up to the formation of the Mishnah (128 in all), the term *tannaim* is applied; and to the students, teachers, and reciters who followed, the term *amoraim*. The Palestinian Talmud was finally redacted at Tiberias

around 400 C.E., and the Babylonian Talmud, which is regarded as the authoritative work, around 500 C.E.

Tanak: Formed from the initial letters of *Torah, Nebi'im, Kethubim*
(i.e., Pentateuch, Prophets, Writings), this is the usual word
among Jews for the Jewish Bible (which is also the Protestant,
but not the Roman Catholic, Old Testament).

Tosephta: A collection of laws parallel to the Mishnah.

Selected Bibliography

Allegro, J. "4 Q Florilegium." *Journal of Biblical Literature* 75 (1956): 176–77; 77 (1958): 350–54.

Al-Tāfahum, 'Abd. "Doctrine." In *Religion and the Middle East*, vol. 2, edited by A. J. Arberry, pp. 365–412. Cambridge: Cambridge University Press, 1969.

Ardrey, R. *The Territorial Imperative*. New York: Atheneum, 1966.

Arendt, H. *The Jew as Pariah: Jewish Identity and Politics in the Modern Age*. Edited by R. H. Feldman. New York: Schocken, 1978.

Avigad, Nahman and Yadin, Yigael. *The Genesis Apocryphon*. Jerusalem: Magnes Press of the Hebrew University, 1956.

Babylonian Talmud, The. 35 vols. London: Soncino, 1935–52.

Barthélemy, D., O.P., and Milik, J. T., et al. *Qumran Cave I: Discoveries in the Judaean Desert*, I. Oxford: Clarendon Press, 1955.

Bennett, W. H. *The Post-Exilic Prophets*. Edinburgh: T. & T. Clark, 1907.

Benoit, Pierre. "Judaïsme et Christianisme." *Revue Biblique* 84 (January 1977): 147–50.

Bickerman, E. J. *Four Strange Books of the Bible*. New York: Schocken, 1967.

———. *From Ezra to the Last of the Maccabees*. New York: Schocken, 1962.

Bonsirven, J. *Le Judaïsme Palestinien*. Paris: Beauchesne, 1934–35.

Bokser, B. M. Review of *The Gospel and the Land* by W. D. Davies. *Conservative Judaism* 30 (1975): 71–74.

Bowman, J. W. *Which Jesus?* Philadelphia: Fortress, 1970.

Brody, H., ed. *Selected Poems of Jehudah Halevi*. Translated by N. Salaman. Philadelphia: Jewish Publications of America, 1924.

Brown, P. *The World of Late Antiquity*. London: Thames & Hudson, 1971.

Brueggemann, W. *The Land*. Philadelphia: Fortress, 1977.

Buber, M[artin]. *Israel und Palestina*. Zurich, 1950. Translated by S. Godman as *Israel and Palestine*. London: East and West Library, 1952.

Buber, Martin, ed. *Jüdische Künstler*. Berlin: Jüdischer Verlag, 1903.

Caquot, A. "Le Rouleau du Temple de Qoumran." *Etudes Théologique* 4 (1978): 443–500.

Charles, R. H., ed. *The Apocrypha and Pseudepigrapha of the Old Testament*. 2 vols. Oxford: Clarendon Press, 1913.

Childs, B. S. *Introduction to the Old Testament as Scripture*. Philadelphia: Fortress, 1979.

Chouraqui, André. *The People and the Faith of the Bible*. Translated by W. V. Gugli. Amherst, Mass.: University of Massachusetts Press, 1975.

Clements, R. E. *Abraham and David*. London: S. C. M. Press, 1967.

Cohen, Hermann. *Die Religion der Vernunft aus den Quellen des Judentums*. Frankfurt: Melzer, 1959.

Condition of Jewish Belief, The. A Symposium Compiled by the Editors of *Commentary* Magazine. New York: Macmillan, 1966.

Cullmann, O. *Christ and Time*. Philadelphia: Westminster, 1950.

Danby, H. *The Mishnah*. Oxford: Oxford University Press, 1933.

Davies, W. D. *The Gospel and the Land: Early Christianity and Jewish Territorial Doctrine*. Berkeley and Los Angeles: University of California Press, 1974.

———. "Israel, Mormons, and The Land." in *Reflections on Mormonism*, edited by T. G. Madsen, pp. 79–97. Provo, Utah: Brigham Young University, 1978.

———. "Paul and the People of Israel." *New Testament Studies* 24 (October 1977): 4–39.

———. "Reflections on the Spirit in the Mekilta: A Suggestion." In *Proceedings of the Sixth World Congress of Jewish Studies*, pp. 159–73. Jerusalem: Hebrew University, 1977.

de Gaulle, Charles. *Memoirs of Hope*. Translated by T. Kilmartin. New York: Simon and Schuster, 1971.

de Vaux, R. "Jerusalem and the Prophets." In *Interpreting the*

Prophetic Tradition, edited by H. M. Orlinsky, pp. 275–300. Cincinnati: Hebrew Union College Press, 1969.

Dillistone, F. W. *Traditional Symbols and the Contemporary World*. London: Epworth, 1973.

Dreyfus, T. "The Commentary of Franz Rosenzweig to the Poems of Jehudah Halevi." *Tarbiz* 47 (March–October 1978): 91 ff.

Eckert, W. P., Levinson, N. P. and Söhr, M., eds. *Jüdische Volk, gelobtes Land*. Munich: Kaiser, 1970.

Finkelstein, L. "Israel as a Spiritual Force." In *Israel: Its Role in Civilization*, edited by M. Davis. New York: Harper, 1956.

———. *New Light from the Prophets*. London: Vallentine, Mitchell, 1969.

———. "Rabbinic Theology and Ethics." In *The Cambridge History of Judaism*, edited by W. D. Davies and L. Finkelstein. Cambridge: Cambridge University Press, forthcoming.

Freedman, D. N. "Divine Commitment and Human Obligation: The Covenant Theme." *Interpretation* 18 (October 1964): 3–15.

———. Review of *The Gospel and The Land* by W. D. Davies. *Journal of Biblical Literature* 95 (1976): 503–6.

Gottwald, N. *The Tribes of Yahweh: A Sociology of the Religion of Liberated Israel, 1250–1050 B.C.E.* Maryknoll, N.Y.: Orbis, 1979.

Goudover, J. van. "Tora und Galut." in *Jüdische Volk, gelobtes Land*, edited by W. P. Eckert, N. P. Levinson, and M. Söhr, pp. 197–202. Munich: Kaiser, 1970.

Halkin, A. S. *Zion in Jewish Literature*. New York: Schocken, 1961.

Halpern, B. *The Idea of the Jewish State*. 2nd ed. Cambridge, Mass.: Harvard University Press, 1969.

Hazleton, L. "The Forgotten Israelis." *New York Review of Books* 27 (29 March 1980): 43–5.

Hertzberg, A. *The Condition of Jewish Belief: A Symposium Compiled by the Editors of "Commentary" Magazine*. New York, 1960.

———. *The French Enlightenment and the Jews*. New York: Columbia University Press, 1968.

———. *The Zionist Idea*. New York: Atheneum, 1968.

Heschel, A. *Israel: An Echo of Eternity*. New York: Farrar, Straus and Giroux, 1969.

Huesman, J. "Archaeology and Early Israel: The Scene Today." *Catholic Bible Quarterly* 37 (1975): 1–16.

Hüttenmeister, F., and Reeg, G. *Die antiken Synagogen in Israel*. *Beihefte zum Tübingen Atlas des Vorderen Orients*, vol. 12. Wiesbaden: Ludwig Reichert, 1977.

Jacob, E. *Israël dans la perspective biblique*. Strasbourg: Editions Oberlin, 1968.

———. "Les Trois Racines d'une théologie de la 'Terre' dans l'A.T." *Revue d'Histoire et de Philosophie Religieuses* 4 (1975): 476–8.

James, M. R., ed. *Liber Antiquitatum Biblicarum*. New York: Macmillan, 1917.

Josephus, Flavius. *Josephus*. Introduction and English translation by H. St. J. Thackery. 8 vols. Loeb Classical Library. New York: G. P. Putnam's Sons, 1926–65.

Kadashin, M. "Aspects of the Rabbinic Concept of Israel." *Hebrew Union College Annual* 19 (1945–46): 57–96.

Katz, J. "The Forerunners of Zionism." *Jerusalem Quarterly* 7 (1978): 10–21.

Kochan, Lionel. *The Jew and His History*. London: Macmillan, 1977.

Kohler, K. "The Testament of Job: An Essene Midrash on the Book of Job, Re-edited and Translated with Introductory and Exegetical Notes." in *Semitic Studies in Memory of Rev. Dr. Alexander Kohut*, edited by G. A. Kohut, pp. 264–295. Berlin: Calvary, 1897.

Lacocque, A. "Une Terre qui découle de lait et de miel." *Vav: Revue de Dialogue* 2 (1966): 28–36.

Lieberman, S. "Response." *Proceedings of the Rabbinical Assembly of America* 12 (1949): 272–89.

Lieberson, Jonathan, and Morgenbesser, Sidney. "The Choices of Isaiah Berlin." *New York Review of Books* 17 (20 March 1980): 30 ff.

Leibowitz, Yehayahu. "State and Religion." *The Jerusalem Quarterly*, No. 14 (Winter 1980), pp. 59–67.

Maier, J. *Die Tempelrolle vom Toten Meer*. Munich: Reinhardt, 1978.

Maimon, Rabbi Moses ben [Maimonides]. *The Guide of the Perplexed*. Translated by S. Pines. Chicago: Chicago University Press, 1963.

Marquardt, F. W. *Die Juden und ihr Land*. Hamburg: Siebenstern–Taschenbuch, 1975.

Mekilta de Rabbi Ishmael. Edited by J. Lauterbach. 3 vols. Philadelphia: Jewish Publication Society of America, 1933–35.

Meyers, Eric M. *Jewish Ossuaries: Reburial and Rebirth*. Rome: Biblical Institute, 1971

Midrash Rabbah. Edited and translated by H. Freedman and M. Simon. 9 vols. London: Soncino, 1939.

Milgrom, J. "The Temple Scroll." *Biblical Archaeologist* 41 (1978): 105–20.

Montague, Ashley. "The New Litany of Innate Depravity, or Original Sin Revisited." In *Man and Agression*, edited by F. Ashley Montague, pp. 3–16. New York: Oxford University Press, 1968.

Moore, G. F. *Judaism*. 3 vols. New York: Schocken, 1971.

Nave, Prina. "Zentrum und Peripherie im Geschichte und Gegenwart." In *Jüdische Volk, gelobtes Land*, edited by W. P. Eckert, N. P. Levinson, and M. Söhr, pp. 82–97. Munich: Kaiser, 1970.

Neher, André. "David Gans (1541–1613), disciple du Maharal de Prague et assistant de Tycho Brahé et de Jean Kepler," *Revue d'Histoire et de Philosophie Religieuses* 52 (1972): 407–414.

———. *L'Existence Juive*. Paris: Editions du Seuil, 1962.

———. *Moses and the Vocation of the Jewish People*. New York: Harper & Row, 1959.

———. *L'Etat'd'Israël: Actes du Collogue Judéo–Chrétien—le Peuple de Dieu, Fevrier 1970*, in *Rencontre–Vav* (Paris, 1972), pp. 74–90.

Neusner, Jacob. "Map Without Territory: Mishnah's System of Sacrifice and Sanctuary." *History of Religions* 19 (November 1979): 103–27.

New English Bible, The. Cambridge and Oxford: Oxford University Press, 1970.

Otto, R. *The Kingdom of God and the Son of Man*. New rev. ed. London: Lutterworth, 1943.

Patterson, D., *The Foundations of Modern Hebrew Literature*. London: Liberal Jewish Synagogue Press, 1961.

———. "Modern Hebrew Literature Goes on Aliyah," *Journal of Jewish Studies* 29 (Spring 1978): 75–84.

Petuchowski, J. J. "Diaspora Judaism—An Abnormality?" *Judaism* 9 (1960): 17–28.

————. *Zion Reconsidered*. New York: Twayne, 1966.

Philo Judaeus. *Philo Judaeus*. Edited and translated by F. H. Colson and G. H. Whitaker. Loeb Classical Library. New York: G. P. Putnam's Sons, 1929–62.

Price, R. E. "A Lexiographical Study of *glh, šbh* and *šwb* in Reference to Exile in the Tanach." Dissertation, Duke University, 1977.

Raitt, T. M. *A Theology of Exile, Judgment and Deliverance in Jeremiah and Ezekiel*. Philadelphia: Fortress, 1977.

Rendtorff, R. *Israel und seine Land*. Munich: Kaiser, 1978.

————. "Die religiosen und geistigen Wurzeln des Zionismus." *Aus Politik und Zeit Geschichte* 49 (4 December 1976): 3–49.

Revised Standard Version of the Bible, The. 2nd ed. New York: Nelson, 1971.

Rotenstreich, Nathan. "Réflexions sur la pensée nationale juive moderne." *Jerusalem Quarterly* 7 (1978): 3–9.

Rowley, H. H. *The Biblical Doctrine of Election*. London: Lutterworth, 1950.

Rubenstein, R. *After Auschwitz. Radical Theology and Contemporary Judaism*. Indianapolis: Bobbs-Merrill, 1966.

Samuel, M. *The World of Scholem Aleichem*. 1945. Reprint, New York: Knopf, 1965.

Sanders, J. A. "Adaptable for Life: The Nature and Function of Canon." In *Magnalia Dei: Festschrift for G. Ernest Wright*, edited by F. M. Cross et al., pp. 531–60. Garden City, N.Y.: Doubleday, 1976.

————. "Text and Canon." *Journal of Biblical Literature* 98 (1979): 5–29.

————. *Torah and Canon*. Philadelphia: Fortress. 1972.

Schaff, Philip. *Creeds of Christendom*. 3 vols. New York: Harper & Row, 1919.

Schmidt, K. L. "Diaspora." In *Theologisches Wörterbuch zum Neuen Testament*, edited by G. Kittel, vol. 2, pp. 98–105. Stuttgart: Kohlhammer, 1935.

Schoffeleers, J. M. *Guardians of the Land: Essays on the Central African Territorial Cults*. Gwelo: Mambo Press, 1979.

Scholem, Gershom. *Jews and Judaism in Crisis*. Edited by W. J. Dannhauser. New York: Schocken, 1976.

Scott, R. B. Y. *The Relevance of the Prophets*. New York: Macmillan, 1968.

Shargel, B. R. "The Evolution of the Masada Myth." *Judaism* 28 (Spring 1979): 357–81.

Shashar, Michael. "The State of Israel and the Land of Israel." *The Jerusalem Quarterly*, No. 17 (Fall 1980), pp. 56–65.

Skinner, J. *Prophecy and Religion*. Cambridge: Cambridge University Press, 1922.

Smith, J. Z. *Map Is Not Territory*. Leiden: E. J. Brill, 1978.

Tal, U. "Historical and Metahistorical Self-Views." In *Religious Zionism*. Tel Aviv: University of Tel Aviv Press, forthcoming.

———. "The Land and the State of Israel in Israeli Religious Life." In *Proceedings of the Rabbinical Assembly*, 76th Annual Convention, 38:1–40. Grossinger, N.Y.: Rabbinical Assembly, 1977.

———. "The Nationalism of Gush Emunin in Historical Perspective." *Forum on the Jewish People, Zionism, and Israel*, no. 36 (Fall/Winter 1979).

Le Talmud de Jerusalem. Translated by M. Schwab. 12 vols. Paris: Librairie Orientale et Americaine, 1932–33.

Thompson, T. L. *The Historicity of the Patriarchal Narratives: The Quest for the Historical Abraham*. New York: W. De Gruyter, 1974.

Urbach, E. E. "Center and Periphery in Jewish Historical Consciousness: Contemporary Implications." In *World Jewry and the State of Israel*, edited by M. Davis, pp. 217–35. New York: Arno, 1977.

Vair, R. J. "The Old Testament Promise of the Land as Reinterpreted in First- and Second-Century Christianity." Dissertation, Graduate Theological Union, Berkeley, 1979.

Van Seters, J. *Abraham in History and Tradition*. New Haven, Conn.: Yale University Press, 1975.

Vaux, R. de. "Jerusalem and the Prophets." In *Interpreting the Prophetic Tradition*, edited by H. M. Orlinsky, pp. 275–300. Cincinnati: Hebrew Union College Press, 1969.

Vermes, G. *The Dead Sea Scrolls in English*. 2nd ed. London: Penguin, 1975.

Vital, D. *The Origins of Zionism*. Oxford: Oxford University Press, 1975.

Von Rad, G. *The Problem of the Hexateuch and Other Essays*. Translated by E. W. T. Dicken. New York: McGraw-Hill, 1966.

Vriezen, T. C. *Die Erwählung Israels nach dem A.T.* Zürich: Zwingli, 1953.

Warren, M. "The Concept and Historic Experience with Land in the Major Western Religious Traditions." In *Proceedings of the Jerusalem Colloquium on Religion, Peoplehood, Nation and Land,* edited by M. H. Tanenbaum and R. J. Zwi Werblowsky, pp. 187–200. Truman Research Institute Publication No. 7. Jerusalem: Hebrew University, 1972.

Werblowsky, R. J. Zwi. "Israël et Eretz Israël," *Les Temps Modernes* 253 (1967) 371–93.

Index of Authors

Subject Index

Designer:	William S. Snyder
Compositor:	Interactive Composition Corporation
Text:	Linotron 202 Bembo
Display:	Linotron 202 Bembo
Printer:	Thomson-Shore, Inc.
Binder:	John H. Dekker and Sons